Sales Magic

Steve Bryant

Published by:
Amherst Media
418 Homecrest Dr.
Amherst, NY 14226
phone/fax 716-874-4450

Proofreader: David Kessler

Cover photo: Matt Murray

ISBN 0-936262-24-9

Library of Congress Catalog
Card Number 92-81809

Printed in the United States of America

Table of Contents

Acknowledgements

First and foremost, this book is dedicated to my customers. Without your patronage, I'd be one very lonely salesman. Thank you for helping me to succeed.

I'd also like to thank the people who believed in me and let me sell in the first place. Thanks to Harry Hallman for encouraging me to push the envelope on all the projects we tackled together. To QVC, my sincere gratitude for giving me the opportunity to sell to over 45 million people every week.

In the world of magic, I'd like to thank my teachers, especially Frank Garcia for his patience with my lack of manual dexterity (and for never using the work "klutz"). Also, my sincere appreciation to Marty Martin and Danny Archer at East Coast Magic, Tony Spina at Tannen's and Hank Lee for opening up a world of possibilities to all of us in the magic community.

Additionally, I'd like to thank Tova Borgnine, Carol Channing, Helen Chen, Nancylee Cranmer, Morgan Fairchild, Susan Lucci, Virginia Olson, Victoria Principal, Joan Rivers, Carol Smith, Dr. Lee Douglas, Bill Fenton, Glen Heckendorf, Reggie Jackson, Graham Kerr, Willie Mays, Vince Pileggi, Paul Prudhomme, Richard Simmons and F. Harrington Smith for letting me see what it's like to sell with the best. Thanks for believing in me!

To my publisher, Craig Alesse of Amherst Media, thanks for sticking with me through the writing of this baby. And thanks for supplying the coffee during the editing ("Are we finished yet?"). And my special gratitude for allowing me to use the techniques outlined in this book to help market it. This way, if people don't buy it, they wouldn't have wanted it anyway.

One final word of appreciation to the men and women who have dedicated their professional lives to sales. Although I pointed out some of our problems in this book, I'm still extremely proud to be one of you!

Preface

Good selling is like good magic. When you make a sale, there is a magical moment not unlike that experienced by a magician who has just amazed an audience. Unlike the performer, however, your rewards are not the immediate applause and appreciation of the crowd. Rather, your payoff is more tangible and much more spendable.

Magicians are very much like salespeople. I know, I've been both...in fact I still am. As a magician, I discovered early-on that the illusions I performed were not all that mysterious — they simply required hard work and study, along with endless practice and refinement. Once I learned them, entertaining audiences was relatively easy.

They thought I was performing miracles. In reality, I was applying the principles I had learned, customizing them to fit my own personality as well as that of my audience. (The latter was always in flux.) One man's magic turned out to be another's set of studied and polished moves.

In sales, I found the same to be true. Once I learned the proper techniques, success was no longer a mystery. Reaching it simply required applying what I had learned to my own style. Since I was accustomed to constantly perfecting my magical abilities, I did the same with my sales skills. While refining these techniques, I discovered that when I took the time to find out how the benefits of my products specifically applied my to customers, my success increased dramatically.

The discovery of the power of these specific benefits led me to define and develop what I call **The Benefit of The Benefit**. It takes the standard sales process to the next level — a level that allows you to succeed while meeting the exact needs of your customers. No illusions...just lots of **real sales magic**!

The new level of sales I've detailed in this text combines elements from both sales and marketing. You'll be working harder — but a lot smarter. The Benefit of The Benefit includes many aspects that were formally the responsibility of marketing, sales support and sales management departments (proposals, sales letters, newsletters, etc.). In the 90's (and beyond) I feel it is necessary for a successful salesperson to integrate these support activities into his or her daily routine.

A lot of work? Yes. Will it pay off? Same answer! Once you begin to use the integrated approach detailed in this book, you'll begin to unravel the many mysteries of great sales. And like me on the day I learned how to do my first card trick, you'll realize that successful sales are no more mysterious than good magic. And you don't even need a top hat and tails.

The ideas in this book will make you a better salesperson. They may also make you angry, since many of them fly in the face of conventional sales wisdom. For one thing, I maintain the days of the sales superstar of the 70's and 80's are gone. Only a few years ago, a super salesperson needed only to sell him or herself — the product was secondary. Dozens of sales books written over the last two decades stressed just that.

The sophistication of the customer in the 1990's has grown to a point where sales professionals need more than an unparalleled product knowledge. Today, we must literally *become* our products. Our knowledge base must increase at all times so that we can keep pace with our customers and the competition.

This enhanced product knowledge will allow us to define the specific benefits (defined as Benefits of The Benefits in this text) of our products for every customer. These specific benefits are the most powerful sales tools I've ever used. They redefine the sales process, making all your efforts work in total harmony in any sales presentation.

My experiences as an advertising copywriter and creative director allowed me to develop the techniques outlined in this book — techniques that I have refined as one of the most successful consumer goods salespeople in the country. My sales total over $200 million in five years, selling directly to the consumer.

Some of the ideas in this book are marketing-based. Others have traditionally been the responsibility of sales managers. A lot of people are going to wonder if the increased workload I'm proposing will be worth the effort. If you want to prosper as a salesperson now and in the future, I feel it is a necessity! If you take control of every aspect of the sales process and do it properly, you will succeed. And once you are in control of every aspect of your success, your earnings potential is unlimited.

In any field, the people who make a difference are those willing to forge new ground and take calculated risks. Selling with the specific benefits outlined in this text, using all the tools at your disposal, going that extra mile (or sometimes more), will make you one of those people. You will be at the top of your field whether you're selling shoes, real estate or multi-million dollar computer hardware systems.

Get ready to suspend some of your established beliefs. I'm proposing many new concepts. I don't expect you to buy into the program right away. However, when you see the achievements of the diverse salespeople cited in this book, I think you'll be as excited as I am about these techniques.

As a one-time professional magician (my experience is noted later in this book), I have come to believe that sales is truly a *magical* process. Throughout the text, I have used several *Magical Interludes* to illustrate some of the important concepts. I hope you'll enjoy them and use the information to work some sales *magic* of your own!

Introduction

Sales is one of those unusual occupations. Unusual, because almost everyone has some dislike for the sales process or the people involved in it. At one time or another we have all said something like, "I hate salespeople. They're too pushy!" Or how about the classic phrase, "Everytime I go to the store, nobody knows anything. All I hear is 'This isn't my department.'"

The dislike for salespeople extends to all regions of the sales community. Have you ever met anyone who has expressed a sincere *love* for a car salesperson? Me neither. In fact, I hate the entire car sales process. (Although I found one auto salesman who is truly exceptional. You'll read about him later in this book.) Many auto salespeople make some of the most common mistakes made in the sales process today. A majority of these folks believe that we love haggling, kind of a throwback to the medieval bazaar. Most think they can sell a car by becoming our friend (in 5 minutes, no less!) and then threatening to end the friendship if we don't sign on the dotted line.

Independent thought? Forget it when it comes to most car sales. These folks run to their "managers" any time the going gets rough. They call this technique a "takeaway." I call it tag team intimidation, a kind of retail version of "good cop, bad cop." If you don't agree to the price quoted by the "bad" salesperson, here comes the "good" manager — who wants to sell you the car at the price you want to pay — as long as you're willing to make a few concessions.

"We can meet your price," says the manager, "by doing away with some of those frills you won't ever need. Driver's side airbag and anti-lock brakes? Hey, you don't want to live if your passengers are splattered all over the road, do you? Think of the endless legal battles. We'll take out that AM/FM cassette deck and install an 18 note Sankyo music box that plays the opening bars of "Feelings." Very soothing in those rush hour traffic jams. Once we remove the automatic overdrive transmission and put in the three speed stick on the steering column, yank off those whitewall tires and replace those leather bucket seats with more practical polyester velvet benches, (adorned with the image of Elvis, no doubt), we'll have no problem meeting your price."

Is it any wonder that most auto makers have been reporting multi-billion dollar losses? With salespeople like that, it's a wonder many of the companies are still in business at all.

Car salespeople aren't alone, however. How many times have you gone to a retail store and asked a question? It's downright laughable. On a recent sojourn to a state-run liquor store in Pennsylvania, I asked where to find the Cabernet Sauvignon. The expression on the clerk's face was similar to what I would imagine you'd see after asking "Is Jimmy Hoffa buried in aisle 3 or 4?"

"The what?!" the clerk with the Hoffaesque expression asked. When I repeated "Cabernet Sauvignon," she tried to repronounce it, creating a word that resembled an utterance heavy metal bands use when they want to say "Satan's the Source" backwards. After this attempt at pronunciation, she said, "This is a liquor store." Although restating the obvious is somewhat of a valid sales technique, somehow I didn't think that's where she was headed.

When I explained that Cabernet was a red wine, she didn't look pleased to realize her error. "That's aisle 4," she snapped. She was right, but there was no sign of Hoffa's grave. Back to the Meadowlands Stadium theory.

Retail sales doesn't pay an exorbitant salary, but you'd think these salespeople would care enough about their jobs to understand the products they sell. Have you ever gone to a department store and asked a product-specific question? Me too. You ever get a straight answer? Me neither.

Many would argue that today's retail clerks are, for the most part, high school and college kids, earning minimum wage. So what?! If they're going to do a sales job, they better realize that stocking shelves and getting back from break on time isn't the entire focus of their job. And, in defense of these fledgling salespeople, their supervisors seem content with their lack of performance, so long as there are warm bodies on the sales floor.

Most of us in the corporate world have dealt with "professional" sales reps who are just as ignorant of the sales process as any 17-year-old working at the mall. In my position at the QVC Network (a nationwide televised shopping channel that reaches more than 42 million people), I had to endure seemingly endless sales presentations from sales reps whose job it was to sell *us,* the show hosts. Never mind that what we needed to know was quite a bit different than the average retail clerk — we got the canned sales pitch. Why? Because that's the only way these people knew how to give a presentation. And our supervisor didn't encourage these people to do otherwise.

Complacency! Laziness! And the "It's just a job" philosophy. These three factors are killing American business. And it has to stop! While this book surely will not be the complete cure, the ideas presented here will show salespeople and managers how to make the most of any sales situation.

Regardless of what products or services you're selling, this book explains many techniques that will allow you to make more sales in less time. These techniques are simple, direct and easy to use in any sales activity. I've developed them through years of experience in the "trenches" while working in advertising and, most recently, as an on-air salesperson for the QVC Network.

When people hear that I have worked for QVC, they always ask the same thing: "How can you talk for three to four hours straight about everything from jewelry to high-tech electronics?" The answer is simple — I follow my own advice. The sales techniques in this book have increased my own sales volume, while allowing me to sound like an expert in virtually any field.

Imagine! Being able to talk with clients (notice I said *with* and not *to*), increasing your credibility with

Section 1:
The Benefit
of The
Benefit

Features, Advantages, Benefits... Then What?

The sales process is most often distilled into three steps: features, advantages and benefits of a product or service. You introduce the product or service (feature), describe it, (advantage) and then describe how it will help your customer (benefit). It boils down to: "This is...which does...which means." Here's a simple example of a features, advantages, benefits type of presentation:

"This is a cordless telephone. It allows you to receieve and make calls within a 1,000 foot range of your home. That means you won't have to make a mad dash for the phone whenever it rings. By using this cordless phone, you'll never have to miss an important call or leave your guests when you need to place one."

Feature, advantage and a few benefits — although somewhat condensed, it's a textbook sales pitch. Years of experience have taught me that this method, while as valid as any, is incomplete. It's a good framework, but with a little extra work, you can make it a powerful weapon by taking it one step further to discover what I define as the Benefit of The Benefit.

A Magical Interlude

If you grew up in the 50's and 60's like I did, you probably remember a Saturday TV show called *The Magic Land Of Alakazam*. Hosted by Mark Wilson, the program was one of the first showcases for magic on American television.

Still, as innovative as it was, Mark had a difficult time convincing TV executives and sponsors that magic would work on TV. Most executives thought the audience would assume that all the effects would be done with "camera tricks." Mark convinced them that he and his cast would issue disclaimers to the contrary throughout the show. He also stressed that the show's live audience would also help to assuage the viewers doubts.

The on-air disclaimers and live audience worked. *The Magic Land of Alakazam* became one of the most popular shows on TV for several seasons. The home audience was obviously dazzled by the magic and convinced that there were no "camera shenanigans" (and there weren't).

Whether he knew it or not, by understanding and addressing the specific needs of the network, Mark was showing them the Benefit of The Benefit of programming his show.

The Benefit of The Benefit

Before you go accusing me of double speak or a feeble attempt at Esperanto, think about those five words. "The Benefit of The Benefit" is really where the benefits of a product or service begin to apply specifically to your customer. Most salespeople are so happy to find a benefit or two, they stop the process right there and jump into a seemingly endless variety of closing techniques. I say that the sales process only **BEGINS** when you identify the benefit.

Take the simple cordless phone example. After hitting the facts and features, you can make a more effective pitch by asking your customer a few questions like, "Do you live in an older home?" If the answer is yes, then you have a benefit of the "never have to miss an important call" benefit mentioned above.

14

By uncovering the fact that your customer has an older home, most of which usually have only one phone jack on the first floor, you can now apply the benefit directly to him or her: "I'll bet you'd love to have a phone jack in every room, like most newer homes. With this cordless model, you really *do* have a phone in every room, because it goes with you. And there's no need to pay the phone company hundreds of dollars to rewire your home. This phone plugs directly into your existing jack and goes wherever you do."

Okay, I'll bet you're asking how I knew that older homes have only one phone jack. Since I once sold cordless phones, I made it my business to find out everything I could about telephones in general. And I mean *everything*! This older home fact was uncovered while reading about the problems the phone companies faced with the divesture of AT&T. Some of the regional operating companies with major rural service areas were faced with the problem of trying to get more phones into homes with older wiring. On the surface, it was a rather dry, relatively uninteresting fact. But sometimes the most insignificant point can help you build an effective sales presentation.

Although I've used a retail example, you'd be surprised how many corporate salespeople don't take the time to find out all they can about their clients. Oh sure, they have an unparalleled understanding about their product or service, but they simply don't take the time to define the specific needs of their prospects.

The Stats of Photostats

Take the case of Charlie, a copier salesperson. Charlie worked 12 to 16 hours a day, very hard, but not very smart. Historically, copier sales have always been a numbers game. You'd start at the top of a high-rise and work your way down, cold calling on every company in the building. Really! You'd hope to come upon a firm whose copier just broke down for the umpteenth time, and pitch the reliability of your machines.

Charlie would usually hit one or two companies per building whose machines had just gone "belly up" during the mid-1980's. Remember, high volume, high-tech copiers were relatively new then, making machine failures fairly commonplace.

Enter the 90's. Not only are copiers much more reliable, but companies have had time to put massive, quick-response sales organizations in place. Add to that our deepening recession and you can understand why Charlie got thrown out on his keister more and more often during these cold calls.

Charlie knew I was in sales and had also worked in advertising. He asked for my advice. I asked him if he knew what type of business was most receptive to his old "pitch after pitch" technique. He didn't know! "It's just a numbers game," he said. "I never cared what business they were in, I just sold them copiers." I fought the urge to ask him to pronounce Cabernet Sauvignon.

When I asked him why the sale of copiers was considered just a numbers game, he responded, "That's the way it's always been. It's the way we've done business from day one." The image of U.S. dollars flying to Japan (and elsewhere) had never been clearer.

Charlie's case is, unfortunately, all too commonplace. Complacency, the "that's the way we've always done it" rhetoric, is probably the single most destructive factor in the sales process. Changing times call for changing tactics. As simple and logical as that sounds, corporate and retail sales organizations alike suffer from this ersatz "if it ain't broke, don't fix it" philosophy.

I suggested to Charlie that he do a little research into the businesses of his prospects. He was resistant at first, but after taking a good long look at his company's recent sales history (or lack thereof), he agreed.

First, we looked at his sales support material; brochures, leave-behinds, etc. Not surprisingly, these were in serious need of updating. His primary brochure was more than two years old and didn't reflect some of the latest models offered by the companies Charlie represented. Working with a local printer, I designed a thin loose leaf binder printed with Charlie's logo. This allowed Charlie to create customized, up-to-date leave-behinds for his prospects. (The design, layout and four color printing cost less than $2,000 for 500 binders.)

Now the tough part — researching the day-to-day business operations of potential clients. The best place to start was with Charlie's existing customer base. He didn't understand why, in a depressed economy, a business would want to spend money on a new copier, when the old one was meeting their needs.

Applying the "Benefit of The Benefit" strategy, we fleshed out a new sales strategy for these existing customers. Here's how it went:

1. **Feature** — A copier creates exact duplicates of documents.

2. **Advantage** — These copies improve both inter- and intra-company communication.

3. **Benefit** — This improved communication will allow the company to grow at a greater rate, improving its bottom line. These better communications would make the company more competitive, a very important point in tough economic times.

4. **Benefit of The Benefit** — (Since this factor changes with every client, I'll use a specific example) One of Charlie's existing customers was an automotive aftermarket sales and service company, replacing and repairing brakes, mufflers, etc. A large portion of the company's business was servicing private and municipal fleets. Charlie's notes indicated that these contracts were extremely competitive and were often terminated on the basis of price alone.

This company used one of Charlie's copiers to reproduce a desktop-generated internal newsletter for other service shops in the chain. We came up with the idea of producing a newsletter for fleet operators. The document would contain informative (and entertaining) features on all aspects of fleet operation. It would take a little work on the part of the automotive service company, but the document would give them an important competitive edge. We even created a mock up of the suggested newsletter, with a few well-researched stories and some money-saving coupons.

It took about half a day to come up with the newsletter idea and the proposal (**see** Section 4: Selling With the Written Word.) Our document cited the benefits of this newsletter and the necessity of having new, faster and more powerful copiers to mass produce it. Bingo! With a little negotiation, Charlie's company had a major sale.

In this case, the benefit of the benefit was "LOSING LESS BUSINESS DUE TO PRICE." Charlie's company was now perceived as a firm sensitive to the automotive aftermarket, one whose advice and counsel would add to the bottom line. His firm went on to establish itself in similar ways with dozens of other businesses. They continue to thrive, even in today's difficult economy. Charlie even hired a full-time marketing director whose job it is to identify "the benefit of the benefit" for new and existing customers.

Salesman, Heal Thyself

I'm sure a lot of you are asking if I really practice what I preach. Absolutely! During my 5 1/2 years as an on-air salesperson for QVC, I produced some of the company's most impressive sales figures by adapting the benefit of the benefit to our sales process.

For those of you who are not familiar with the QVC (Quality, Value and Convenience) Network, it employs an informational (as opposed to a hard sell) approach to sales. QVC uses articulate show hosts to present products in a "video catalog" type of presentation. The medium offers a great deal of latitude for personal initiative and creativity.

Take the case of a particular line of skin care products. Sales for the line were good and, once we had an imbedded base of customers to provide on-air testimonials, they were getting even better. With sales increasing, why try to rock the boat by introducing something new? Simply stated, when sales are good, that's the best time to make them better. Remember the old axiom, "Nothing succeeds like success?" Nothing could be more correct!

Too often, salespeople pull back their efforts when things are good. The whole concept of The Benefit of the Benefit is pushing the envelope, finding factors that will make your product or service irresistible.

I had a potential audience of tens of millions on QVC. To increase sales effectively, I had to identify a benefit of the benefit for one on-air telephone caller that would apply to a majority of viewers. During one presentation, I had a caller who, from her comments, obviously had a full-time job during the week. Since this meant she probably had some type of regular commute, I asked her if spent a lot of time in a car (a bus or train would have been as effective).

The caller replied that she drove to and from work 5 days a week. Since I had done some research and discovered that the air from a car heater was very drying and harsh to the skin, I told her that it was doubly good that she was using the product. She replied that she hadn't thought about the drying air in her car but was glad to know it. (Remember, I really wasn't selling her since she was already a customer. I was trying to identify a common benefit of the benefit for a large group of people.) I also added facts about the forced hot air in other forms of mass transportation to our on-air chat.

Within a few moments of this discussion, the phone lines lit right up. It was the middle of a Saturday afternoon, not one of the hottest TV sales times, and yet I had one of the most successful airings for the product that weekend.

Here's the logic I used to arrive at this particular Benefit of the Benefit:

1. *Feature* — This is an all-natural skin care system that's fast and easy to use.

2. *Advantage* — It helps your skin to maintain a healthy, youthful appearance.

3. *Benefit* — You will look better (to yourself and other people) and feel better by using the product.

4. *Benefit of The Benefit* — HOW MUCH BETTER YOU WOULD FEEL AND YOUR SKIN WOULD LOOK AFTER USING THE PRODUCT TO COUNTERACT THE ADVERSE CONDITIONS THAT EXIST IN A COMMON SITUATION. The testimonial calls already established that the product worked, I merely applied the benefit to a situation that would apply to a large group of people.

It took a little extra time on my part to find out which environmental conditions were the toughest on skin, but it paid off. I also uncovered some facts about sun exposure and was ready to explore those if we had any callers from the sun belt. We didn't, but I was "locked and loaded" for the next time.

Remember, I did this research on my own, at a time when sales on this particular product were very high. Too often, salespeople wait until sales are bad before they give any extra effort. Many times that's too late. Think about your sales failures. Did you try anything to help increase business when things were good? Don't feel bad; most people don't want to "rock the boat" when things are fine.

By maximizing your efforts when sales seem to be at their zenith, you are coming from a position of strength. If you are playing the role of "firefighter" because things aren't going well, you will always have one or more obstacles to overcome before you can get to the business of selling.

Winning a Losing Battle

Along with this skin care product, I was often called upon to sell a popular weight loss plan on QVC. Sales numbers for the plan were consistently good. Still, I spent some time trying to come up with ways to make them better.

I didn't have to look too far. I had worked for QVC for more than four years at that point. Four sedentary, physically inactive years that had packed an extra 20 pounds on my 5'11" frame. My shirts were tight, my jackets pulled and the pleats in my slacks had been stretched smooth. My tailor suggested that I go to a 44 regular suit since he was running out of material to let out. It was time to find out just how effective this plan was.

It amazes me how many salespeople don't use their own products or services. How many times have you gone to a hair stylist whose own coif looked a lot like Elsa Lanchester's in *Bride of Frankenstein*? How about the clothing salesperson who looks like an ad for the 70's Polyester Look Comeback Tour? And let's not forget the outside computer salesperson who knows his or her product inside and out but doesn't own or carry a laptop or notebook computer.

Personal testimonials are some of the most effective sales techniques in existence. They also offer one of the easiest paths to establish "benefits of benefits." And regardless of what your company is selling, there is most often a way to use it yourself. If you're asking "Why would I ever use _____?," about your own product or service, then maybe it's time to open up that little roadside Elvis museum you've always wanted.

I tried the plan. It worked! 15 pounds came off in a month and I was rarely hungry. While I didn't care for the exercise videos that came along with it (I've never liked to exercise alone), I went back to the gym to get the regular exercise I needed to tighten up and maintain the loss. I even lost the additional 5 pounds without trying, since Deal-A-Meal had taught me how to eat correctly, without reaching for the peanut butter jar every hour. (Thank heavens! Do you have any idea how silly it would have looked to check into the Betty Ford Clinic for a peanut butter addiction?)

Wow! I had an undeniable personal testimonial. My clothes fit again and the pleats were back in my pants. I sat down (pleats still there) and wrote out a way to make this Benefit of The Benefit work in my next presentation. It occurred to me that the majority of taped and live testimonials we used on-air were from people who had lost hundreds of pounds. My success had defined an entire new market (especially where the QVC audience was concerned): people with a middle-aged spread who had a few pounds of "happy fat" (is there also "sad thin?") to lose.

Things went better than I expected. The next time I sold the weight loss plan, I did the usual presentation with the really seriously overweight people and then dropped my "bombshell." Showing my loose jacket and the well defined pleats in my pants, I announced my personal success. Since I had taken the time to make some notes on my day-to-day experiences, (QVC is mostly ad libbed), the story flowed extremely well. Like the previously mentioned skin care system, as soon as I identified a new Benefit of the Benefit, the phones lit up.

Again, to find The Benefit of the Benefit, I did a simple features, advantages, benefits chart.

1. *Feature* — This is a weight control system that will help a severely overweight person to safely and effectively lose weight.

2. *Advantage* — You will lose weight with little effort and also keep the weight off.

3. *Benefit* — When you are no longer severely overweight, you will be healthier, look and feel better and have a more positive image of yourself. (Obviously, there are literally dozens of benefits for this plan.)

4. *Benefit of The Benefit* — HOW GOOD I FELT AND LOOKED AFTER LOSING ONLY 20 POUNDS BY USING THIS WEIGHT LOSS PLAN.

Without "hamming it up," I described how much I was able to accomplish now that I had more energy due to the weight loss and regular exercise. I also talked about how, even though it was unfair, I was much more accepted in social situations after slimming down. These facts made the plan more attractive to people who did not have to lose the more substantial amounts of weight usually associated with the program.

This presentation was the most successful airing of the weekend, grossing over $660,000 in thirty minutes. I am proud to say that even after my initial revelation, the best sales results for the plan occurred during my shows, again using slight variations of this particular Benefit of the Benefit.

A Magical Interlude

One of the greatest stage magicians of the Twentieth Century, Harry Blackstone Sr., had one very famous occasion when he really had to use his own "products." During one of his performances, he was quietly informed that the theater was ablaze and the fire was out of control. The building had to be evacuated, without panicking the audience.

Blackstone took a deep breath, thought a moment, then calmly informed the crowd that he was going to perform the most astounding effect he had ever attempted...but they would have to follow him outside to witness it. He was using his "products" — magic, illusion and showmanship — trying to convince his audience as well as himself that everything was status quo.

The spectators obediently left the building, eager to see the promised miracle. Blackstone was the last to leave. Just as he stepped outside, the facade of the theater erupted into flames, becoming completely engulfed in a matter of moments. The audience was safe and sound and thoroughly convinced that the man had performed one of the greatest illusions they had ever witnessed. It was only the next day when they saw the charred remains of the building that most of them realized Blackstone's quick thinking and complete command of his craft had saved hundreds of lives.

"Selling" Clothes Can Make The Man

This is one of my favorite stories in the book. Although it is based in retail sales, it has served as an inspiration for me in many different sales situations.

John was a high school graduate in the New Orleans area. His first full-time job was in a men's clothing store, a national chain located in a major shopping mall. He was bright, ambitious and a quick study, which is why his boss left him alone in the store on one of his first days on the job.

It was 8:30 on a Saturday night and the mall was very quiet. John's boss, eager to get home to family and TV, gave John the task of closing the store at 9:00. At about 8:45, a man came in wanting to look at some new suits. He needed a new navy blue suit for his daughter's wedding. He was the only customer in the store and John (the only remaining employee at this time) helped him to pick out a excellent quality single-breasted garment.

While John was marking the suit for alterations, the man explained that his daughter's wedding was at 2:00 PM...THE NEXT DAY! He stated that he knew it was last minute but he would gladly pay *any* overtime charges to have the store's tailors alter the suit that night.

John explained that the store didn't have its own tailors and that the earliest he could get the suit was Monday afternoon and even that would entail rush charges. The man reiterated his situation, explaining that he was a very busy professional, prone to procrastination in his personal life (also implying that he was a master of understatement) and, like most men, hated to shop. He knew that it was last minute, but he needed the suit tomorrow and would pay whatever it cost to accomplish that.

At 8:55 PM on Saturday night, John began to make phone calls. He first called other clothing stores that had in-house tailor shops. Even after hearing the phrase "money is no object," the stores were unreceptive. A few even hung up when they realized that John was calling from "the competition."

John could see that the man was feeling bad about waiting so long to find a suit as well as having the misfortune to shop in a store that didn't have its own tailor. After the phone response John had received, he wondered if any of the stores who had tailors would have cared enough to help the man.

Letting "his fingers do the walking," John called all the independent tailors in the vicinity. He left messages on several phone machines but realized it would probably be Monday morning before anyone would hear them.

Since the alteration marks on the garment could be easily removed, John had the option of canceling the sale and sending his customer away, secure in the fact that there was no solution to the problem. How many of us would be tempted to do the same? To most salespeople, unfortunately, it would seem like the only logical course of action.

John wanted the sale (over $500) and really got into the spirit of the challenge. He explained to the man that chances of getting the suit altered that night were slim, but he would give it his best try. The man reiterated that he would pay whatever it cost and handed John $200 in cash to cover the last minute alterations.

As the man left the store, John felt some sense of panic. He knew that store policy forbade him to seek another alteration shop. What if he failed to have the suit altered that night and his boss found out? What if, by the largest stroke of luck, he could get the suit altered, but the alterations were done poorly? His enthusiasm began to wane, but he began to consider the situation carefully.

John asked himself what was open in and around New Orleans after 9:00 PM on a Saturday night? Then it hit him — THE FRENCH QUARTER! And while, as a resident, John hadn't visited the tourist area in years, he figured that the Bourbon St. area was his best bet. He put the suit in a bag and headed off for the home of blackened food and Dixieland.

Bourbon St. was alive with activity. Many clubs advertised "Open 24 Hours," but there were no all night tailoring shops in sight. John walked the length of Bourbon St., and all its side streets, for over 2 hours until he found a little fortune teller's shop with a hand written sign that read: "Tarot Cards Read, Palmistry, Voodoo Spells Broken, Custom Tailoring." He walked in.

The shop looked exactly as we would all imagine. Dark, dingy and dusty with a card table and two chairs. The thin, craggy-faced woman sitting at the table looked at John and began to tell his fortune. John interrupted and told her that he needed a suit altered that night.

"Cost you extra to get it that quick," she replied. "Lots extra!" John asked how much, figuring her fee could dwarf the $200 he was carrying. The woman examined the markings on the suit, thought for a few moments and replied, "$25.00!"

John was shocked and she obviously mistook his silence for disapproval. "$20.00," she snapped, "but no less." John quickly agreed.

The woman finished the suit in a little over an hour. John was so impressed with the quality of her workmanship he "tipped" her $5.00. Not waiting for the predictions she was obviously throwing in for free, John headed home.

The next morning, John called the man, who came immediately to the store and picked up his suit. The man was so impressed that he told John to keep the remaining $175 dollars from the alteration "fund" for his trouble.

While John's boss was a trifle upset by John's freelance efforts, any misgivings faded when the man, a major mover and shaker in the New Orleans business scene, returned to the store in a few days to purchase a new wardrobe worth over $5,000. He was so impressed with John's efforts that he recommended the store to many of his peers. Business was booming, especially in high-end men's suits.

So how does THE BENEFIT OF THE BENEFIT fit into this scenario? Here it comes:

From conversations with his new upper echelon clientele, John became aware of one common fact — MOST MEN HATE TO SHOP FOR CLOTHES! ESPECIALLY BUSY, SUCCESSFUL MEN. John decided to make this work for him. He studied all he could about alterations and became so skillful that he could mark up a suit once he had someone's measurements.

Once a customer had been fitted by John, he need never return to the store. One visit was all it took. After that, all somebody had to do was call John and tell him what colors and styles he wanted. To make things as easy as possible for his customers, John arranged to have the suits delivered to his clients at work or home.

Soon, John would make outbound calls, informing his customers of new styles, colors and fabrics. He could sell an entire seasonal wardrobe on the phone. He had become so skilled at marking clothes for alterations that he could even adjust for most weight gains or losses without having to mark the garment on the person. John and his store became known as the place to shop if you didn't have time or didn't like to shop. A place that could meet impossible deadlines.

Working on commission, John's salary rose to the six figure range. He used a personal computer to keep track of his customers. Within a few years, his commissions had elevated his salary to beyond that of the company's CEO (before stock options and perks). He parlayed his increased earnings into a college education for himself and, although now retired from clothing sales, he remains very active as a businessman and investor.

By identifying the fact that most men hate to shop, John identified an extraodinarily powerful Benefit of the Benefit.

Without realizing it, he went through a well-thought-out features, advantages, benefits track.

1. *Feature* — This is a new wardrobe.

2. *Advantage* — You will look good and in style by wearing these clothes.

3. *Benefit* — When you wear these clothes, you will feel good about yourself and people will perceive you as being successful.

4. *Benefit of the Benefit* — HAVING ALL THE BENEFITS OF A NEW WARDROBE WITHOUT MAKING REPEATED TRIPS TO THE STORE.

If he hadn't given an extraordinary effort in the first place, this fact might have gone undiscovered. Sometimes, a little extra effort and innovation is all that separates extremely successful salespeople from mediocre performers.

A Magical Interlude

The psychic entertainer The Amazing Kreskin always has his paycheck hidden somewhere in the theater where he is performing. He agrees that if he can't find it using his psychic skills, he will forfeit his salary. In the thousands of performances he has done all over the world, he has only failed to find the check three times.

While audiences are awed by his apparent display of *Extrasensory Perception*, Kreskin is quick to admit that he doesn't have traditional ESP, but rather what he calls Extremely "Sensitive" Perception. He uses his knowledge of human nature and his highly trained skills of observation to perform what appear to be miracles of mind reading.

Kreskin acknowledges that anyone could astound audiences the way he does if he or she were willing to put in the time necessary to learn how to develop this heightened awareness of the human condition. Few, if any, have ever been willing to make this commitment.

The Laughing Software Salesman

Computer software: the instructions that tell a computer what to do, like process words, crunch numbers and the like...sounds dry at best, right? That's what the industry thought for years. Sales presentations for computer software had always been very businesslike, straightforward and downright dull.

When a computer software company came to an ad agency I worked for prior to joining QVC, the first thing I did was ask how theirs and other programs had been marketed in the past. They told us that most companies used printed flip charts explaining exactly how their systems worked. Each page of the flip chart showed a different feature of the system (no benefits, just features). Since their system (a program that helped programmers develop new programs) had over 100 different features, they used over 100 flip charts. Perhaps dull was too kind a word.

The presentation took over 2 hours! I fell asleep (along with our VP of design and sales manager) while they were giving it. We hoped they hadn't noticed. Through stifled yawns, we began to analyze the situation. Since none of us had ever worked with computer software before, we immediately worked up several features, advantages, benefits charts. We felt this one held the most promise:

1. *Feature* — This is a computer software package which allows programmers to develop and keep track of new programs. (This was condensed from 100 separate fea-

tures, all agonizingly detailed on an equal number of flip charts.)

2. *Advantage* — The system is easy to use and secure.

3. *Benefit* — By using the system, programmers are more productive and can create more programs in less time, resulting in greater profits for their companies.

4. *Benefit of The Benefit* — In this case, the benefit of the benefit we used for the sales presentation was virtually the same as a benefit of the product itself: SAVE TIME (AND MONEY) WHILE WATCHING A PRESENTATION ABOUT A NEW SOFTWARE PROGRAM THAT WILL SAVE YOUR COMPANY TIME AND MONEY.

In this case, we didn't use the specific needs of the end user to define the Benefit of the Benefit. Since we found out the decision maker wasn't the programmer, but usually a top executive who had little computer experience, we tailored this aspect accordingly (and remember, the old sales pitch was a highly detailed, 2 hour flip chart affair laden with computerese).

Since the software program was real cutting edge technology, saving the company time and money, we decided to use an equally new state-of-the-art technology to convey this message. We proposed a video presentation using actual computer screens showing the program in action. And, we decided to make the video FUNNY!

They flipped out! Humor in a serious business presentation...no one ever did that! When we pointed out that their software was equally "trend-setting," they softened to the idea. Anyway, they had noticed that we had fallen asleep during their presentation and figured if a vendor dozed off, a prospective client would probably reach delta sleep.

Here's how we explained the Benefits of The Benefits as they applied in this situation: First and foremost, the video presentation would stress the benefits of the software — something their flip charts neglected to do. It would be produced using an impressionist doing the voices of Jack Benny (detailing how the software saved *time* and *money)*; George C. Scott as General Patton, (explaining how it was a secure system); Howard Cosell, noting the "teamwork" aspects of the program); and George Burns, telling the audience about the long life of the system.

Once the video was produced, it would be sent to prospective clients in a new, portable, self-contained VCR and TV. It would arrive with a colorful one page explanation and even a bag of microwave popcorn. The shipping case would even contain all the necessary labels for returning the unit. Keep in mind, it would only be sent to prospects who had been pre-qualified on the telephone, the same folks who would have been targeted for that "lethal" flip chart presentation.

Since the video didn't require an on-site salesperson (until the prospect was sufficiently intrigued by the video) the software company could now make dozens more initial presentations each month. We had created a high tech, easy-to-understand and fun presentation for a high tech, easy-to-understand and fun (from a programmer's standpoint) software program.

The video presentation was a hit. The company experienced a phenomenal growth in sales. So much so that they attracted the attention of a huge national conglomerate who bought them out, making the principals of the software company very wealthy men.

Prior to this incident, I didn't know anything about computer software. During the entire process, I took the time to hit the library and become conversant with the subject. Understanding as much as you can about a product or service will really help your sales performance. You'd be surprised how few people really take the time to fully understand what they're selling.

The More (Information), The Merrier

It is much easier to define The Benefit of the Benefit when you really understand even the most minute details about what you are selling. I don't mean just a cursory understanding, but an in-depth knowledge rivaling experts in the field. Impossible? No! Difficult? Yes, but manageable.

Prior to the computer software marketing plan, I had no concept of what software was or what it did. (This was in the early 80's when even word processors were luxurious mysteries for most of us.) When I first heard about it, I thought it was some magnificent machine that you plugged into your computer. It was easier to think of it that way, as a tangible commodity.

When our sales director explained that it was a set of binary instructions, read from a disk, I knew it was time to hit the library. Even in the early 80's, there were several shelves of computer software books. At first, I was lost. I took several texts to a desk and started to peruse. It was like trying to decipher Sanskrit or Aramaic. As the subject was still fairly new and extremely specialized, even the research librarian couldn't help me. With only two days until the client meeting, I hit upon an information gathering formula that I use to this day.

I made several calls to local colleges and universities and spoke with several professors of computer science. I asked them for recommendations on *basic* books about computer software. They were extremely helpful and suggested quite a few books.

Two of the books they recommended were available at the main branch of the Philadelphia Library. (Main branches in large metropolitan areas are your best bet.) I checked them out and set upon a course of study.

Since I needed a crash, college-level course, I took a few hours before cracking the books and made up an exam full of information I would have to know before our first client meeting. Without this knowledge, I could have made some crucial errors in the initial meeting, like asking if the software came in colors or if there was a more durable model, something like hard-software. Not just egg on my face, but an entire omelet with a side of Canadian bacon awaited if I didn't know my stuff.

Once my sample exam was ready, I hit the books. Since our agency was very busy, this research had to be done on my own time, in the evening. I must admit, there were (and still are, for that matter) times when HBO or a racquetball game at the local gym called out loud and clear during the cram sessions. Hey, I was a creative director. That wonderful rationalization machine we all have in our brains was screaming "This isn't your job! Let the client bring you up to speed. You're quick on your feet. You can fake it!"

How many times have we all heard, "YOU'RE SELLING THE SIZZLE, NOT THE STEAK." That's true, but if you don't know how to turn on the stove, you're in deep trouble.

I kept a log of the research time (I still do) just to see how much effort I put into the project. By the time the client meeting rolled around, I had spent 10 hours of my "off time" in two days. But during the first meeting, I made quite an impression on the client. In fact, during subsequent meetings their president told me that they had chosen our agency since we really knew software. They were concerned about our very creative approach, but my "knowledge" of the subject helped to put them at ease.

It's crucial to remember that you must never lie about your expertise in a field. Ever! When the folks at the software company asked how I knew so much, I told the truth. I told them I spent some time over the last two days reading up on the subject to make sure our agency could properly service their account. If I had tried to pass myself off as an expert, I could have never asked the extensive questions I did during the initial script research. Once people realize you are doing your best to understand their business, they'll bend over backwards to help you out. Get caught in a lie, no matter how small, and you'll never regain their respect (or their future business for that matter).

Research Etiquette

Whenever I tapped a fellow professional for research, I always took the time to send him or her a note of thanks. In the note I also offered my assistance should it ever be needed. You'd be surprised how well this worked. I actually built many professional friendships that served as my own personal database/think tank. In my conversations with many of these people, I was shocked at how many others had come to them for help and never taken the time for a simple written thank you.

(In the 1990's and beyond, personal research sources will continue to be valuable. But don't overlook Compuserve, Prodigy and the other computer databases that are available. They are also an excellent source of information and most cost less than $200 per year to join. Their information runs the gamut from complete on-line encyclopedias to product and service-specific databases.)

So how does in-depth research apply if you are involved in a more direct selling situation, either in the field or even a retail situation? Let me explain with another example.

A Little Knowledge Goes A Long Way

I know a retail electronics salesperson. Sara always outperformed her peers. In an industry where $40,000 to $50,000 per year is a terrific salary, she consistently pulled down over six figures every year.

With no background in electronics, did she become an overnight expert in audio and video equipment? Yes and no.

Sara realized that most folks buying high-tech audio and video gear fit into two categories: People with great technical knowledge (either real or supposed) and those who feared their lack of knowledge. Either category did not truly want an expert salesperson. If you doubt me, just strike up a conversation with an audiophile or video buff. Make one absolute statement and get ready for a lengthy argument.

Rather than set herself up as an expert, Sara read as much as she could. She borrowed some books from the library, bought a few others for permanent reference and subscribed to several consumer and industry publications. (The latter two are totally tax deductible).

Armed with a good stock of electronics knowledge, Sara hit the sales floor. As a novice to the arena, she watched her peers and saw two distinct approaches. One group of salespeople were literal experts. Their knowledge was flawless and they delighted in entering into lengthy technical discussions with customers. The knowledgable customers would argue fact after pointless fact, often killing an hour before any sales decision would be made.

The other salespeople weren't equipment savvy, but were virtual warehouses of knowledge about audio and video releases (CDs, audio and video tapes and laser discs). They used the "sizzle" of the equipment, applying it to the customer's area(s) of interest. If the customer was shopping for a stereo and liked rock music, these "software intensive" salespeople would engage them in discussions of the latest groups and solo artists. For the VCR or laser disc shopper, they would do their best Siskel and Ebert impression and review current and classic films available in the various media.

Even though this latter group was closer to defining the benefits of their products than the "technophile salespeople," they were still injecting opinions where they weren't needed. These folks, like the former group, used their knowledge as a weapon. They wanted to impress the customers with their knowledge and tried to come off as experts in the field of music and cinema. Again, endless discussions where the salesperson played the role of the superior, becoming a preacher, not a teacher. A lot of wasted sales time.

Although both types of salespeople were making a living, Sara decided to use her knowledge in a different, and what she hoped would be a more productive, manner. When she engaged in a conversation with a technically savvy customer, she allowed him or her to take the lead. She would usually know more than the "expert" standing in front of her, but she never let them know it. And, most importantly, she did something her peers truly neglected to do — she listened!

If any erudite customers had a specific brand loyalty, she would listen and make recommendations to meet their needs within the favored brand. If their needs didn't mesh with that brand, she would try to guide them gentlyto a more suitable one. However, if she met with any serious resistance, she would yield to their preference, doing her best to match them to a piece of equipment that came as close as possible to satisfying their requirements.

With customers who had little or no knowledge of the equipment they wanted, she played the role of teacher. She gently coached her neophyte customers on what was available and, once their specific needs surfaced, she would guide them to the equipment that was right for them. If any brand loyalty was apparent, she did her best to match their needs to the brand.

Her co-workers flipped! Imagine, giving the customer what he or she wanted without using her superior knowledge to match them to the "equipment of their dreams." Many even complained to management that the young lady was giving the store a bad name by "knuckling under" to the demands of the customers.

Initially, Sara actually took some heat from her superiors for her "unorthodox" approach. However, when her sales figures were consistently nearly double that of the next highest producer, management backed off. Additionally, her return rate (equipment brought back for refund or exchange) was almost nil. Add to that dozens of letters from happy customers (all of whom lauded her in-depth knowledge) and you can understand why Sara was given the opportunity to manage a store after less than a year with the chain.

Without formally defining it, Sara was using The Benefit of the Benefit. If her customers wanted a stereo, VCR, or whatever, Sara would USE HER KNOWLEDGE OF THE PRODUCT TO FIND OUT HOW THE GENERAL BENEFITS OF THE AVAIL-

ABLE UNITS WOULD *SPECIFICALLY* APPLY TO HER CUSTOMERS. And she did it while making them feel good about the entire process. Today, she is an Executive Vice President with the chain, and has organized sales training based on her experiences "in the trenches."

As a matter of fact, Sara did one additional thing that really set her apart from her peers: She kept copious notes on all her sales encounters — which techniques worked, which ones didn't, which approaches worked the best on different types of customers, etc.

Her notes provided the basis for the sales training program she established in her company. Mine became the outline for this book. I really do practice what I preach.

A Magical Interlude

The great stage magician of the 19th Century, Robert-Houdin (from whom Eric Weiss derived the name "Houdini"), was a watchmaker until he took up magic at the age of 40. An enterprising man, he was always looking for new and innovative ways to use his watchmaking knowledge.

The skill and expertise he developed in his first career allowed him to create astounding mechanical illusions for his performing endeavors. These automatons included a mechanical orange tree that actually "grew and bore fruit" in a matter of seconds!

This dramatic effect gave Houdin a reputation as a man who possessed unnatural and extraordinary powers. In reality, he was just an accomplished watchmaker with a great sense of showmanship and a desire to find innovative applications for his expertise.

A Word About Customer Service

As you have probably noticed by now, The Benefit of The Benefit — finding out how general benefits specifically apply to a customer — is really based upon customer service. The more you service and meet the needs of your customers — the more likely you are to uncover and define The Benefit of The Benefit. Since this applies whether you are selling cars, shoes, vacuum cleaners or jet aircraft, I thought the following customer service (or lack thereof) scenario would be of interest.

While working on this book, I had the occasion to be in a retail jewelry store. I was having a ring sized. (The weight loss plan I had sold on QVC even reduced my fingers.) While waiting for the work to be done, I witnessed the following:

A young (early twenties) man walked into the store and asked to see some engagement rings.

"What kind of cut do you want on the stone?" the clerk asked.

The young man timidly replied, "I don't know, I'm kind of new at this."

The clerk didn't even crack a smile. "Well, how much do you want to spend?" He sounded a little annoyed.

"Well, I don't know. Like I said, I'm new at this." The young man seemed really embarrassed about his lack of knowledge.

"Look," the clerk snapped, "I have to have more information or I can't help you!"

The young man (along with myself) was shocked. "If I could just see a few different types and prices, I'd have a better idea." His voice was trembling, he was obviously upset.

"I'm sorry," replied the unsympathetic clerk, "I just can't take the time to show you hundreds of rings until you find the one you want." (I was the only other customer in the store.) "Check your finances and bring in your fiancee and we'll try to fix you up." The clerk busied himself with some paperwork, signaling to the young man that their conversation had ended.

AND RETAIL JEWELERS WONDER WHY THE CABLE SHOPPING INDUSTRY IS KICKING THEIR TEETH DOWN THEIR THROATS?!!!

I took the time to follow the young man outside and, with the knowledge of jewelry I've gained while working at QVC, tried to help him out. It seems that he hadn't popped the question yet and that the ring was going to be a surprise for his fiancee-to-be. He had been saving for almost two years and had scraped together a little over $3,000 for the ring. Even at full retail, that will buy a dandy ring. Since QVC didn't really specialize in engagement rings, I sent him to a jeweler I had dealt with in the past — one that prided itself in customer service as well as a fine selection of diamond engagement rings. I followed up. The young guy dropped $3,000+ on a lovely one carat solitaire. I wish them well.

As for the offending store, boy did they step in it. Not only did they blow a $3,000 sale (unforgivable at any time, especially when consumer dollars are tight), they also lost me as a customer and bought more bad word-of-mouth publicity than they could have ever imagined.

If the jeweler had only asked the young man to sit down, offered him some coffee and spent less than five minutes with him, he would have realized a $3000 sale, right on the spot. (The young man had the cash in his pocket.) With the triple or better markup that's standard in the jewelry industry, we're talking at least a $2,000 profit.

Whenever I think about blowing a sale, I must admit that the recent adventures I had while trying to purchase a new car rank right up there. Of course, there are also some terrific car salespeople who, knowingly or not, use The Benefit of The Benefit regularly. Which brings us to a section I call...

It Was The Best of Sales, The Worst of Sales...

For two years, I squeezed my late 30's frame into a little two-seater sports car. It was great, until I hit 40. Then it was time for a "grownup car" (or so my sacroiliac was telling me). Since my last book had done rather well, I decided to treat myself to my first "luxury vehicle." (To me, that's where they don't charge you extra for the FM radio or whitewalls.) Off to that last bastion of blood-and-guts selling: the new car dealership.

Since it had only been two years since I had gone through this ordeal, I still had a few scars and nasty memories. I decided to take some of my own advice and become an educated consumer. I read several consumer guides about which new cars would allow you to survive a head-on crash with the Chrysler Building and didn't cost as much as the national debt of a third world country. There were actually quite a few in my price range, all with FM and whitewalls as standard equipment.

Off to the first dealer. I walked in and was immediately faced with The Land of The Lost. The salespeople hadn't sold a car in so long they were sitting around trading poverty stories. Really! I overheard snippets of conversations about making mortgage payments, paying college tuition...it was like a microcosm of bad luck stories. Boy, was I going to be able to strike a bargain with these people. They'd probably *give* me the car if I could just buy the gas to get it off the lot.

Even with the poverty tales I heard, it still took several minutes for a salesperson to approach me. (I was the only customer in the place.) Then, she asked me the stupidest question in the world of sales. Stupid, yes, but we've all used it. "Can I help you?" A yes or no question, right out of the gate!!! I had already won. These people were bozos. I could have them eating out of my hand in a few minutes.

"Yes," I replied. "I'm interested in your luxury sedan. I really like the white one right outside the showroom."

"I don't have the keys for that one," she said. "My manager has them and I don't know when he'll be back. But I do have the keys to the red one. It's almost the same, just a different engine."

"How different?"

"It's a four cylinder engine. The white one has a six."

"I'm really interested in the six."

"I don't have the keys to the white six. But the red is essentially the same car."

"Essentially?" I asked.

"Well, the white six has a leather interior. The red has cloth. And the red is a stick, the white is an automatic."

"Interesting sub-definition of essentially," I added.

"Would you like to test drive the red four?" There was no emotion in her voice. It had either been burned out by years of sales inactivity or she was just a dolt.

"Okay, I'll test the red four. If I really hate it, then I'll probably love the white six."

"That's a good way to look at it," she replied. (I swear I'm not making any of this up.)

As I got in the red four and closed the door I was struck by two things. First of all, the door closed with a resonant, loud thud. It sounded very solid. Secondly, my head hit the roof. When I asked her how to adjust the seat to avoid severe vertebrae compression in my neck and upper back, she looked annoyed.

"I'll have to get out and do it from your side," she snapped. Hey, for $30,000+, she should get the National Corps of Engineers to adjust it.

Once she was on my side, it took her over a minute to find the height adjustment control. Then, after a few minutes of finagling, she promptly announced, "That's as low as it goes."

"But my head is still hitting the ceiling."

(Again, I swear the following is absolutely true.) "You'll get used to it. Every car has its own personality."

After calmly explaining that I had an obvious personality conflict with the vehicle, I excused myself and drove off the lot with a new appreciation for my little two-seater.

There are 8 million stories in the Naked City, and nearly as many in my search for the perfect new car. I found more bad salespeople than there were VW Beetles on the road in 1968. Countless "good cop, bad cop" scenarios alluded to in the introduction of this book. But finally, I found a salesperson who asked me the finest opening question I've ever encountered while shopping for a car (or probably anything else).

"Where will you be driving it most often?" he asked as I was ogling a pure white beauty on the lot. His smile was convincing and, unlike many salespeople I've dealt with in retail and other situations, he was immaculately clean and sharply dressed.

I beamed at the question. "Where will you be driving it most often?" In 8 words, he cut through the BS and put me in the situation of providing him with The Benefit of the Benefit with my answer. Even if this wasn't the car for me, any semblance of a thoughtful answer on my part would give him most (if not all) the information he needed to sell me a car.

"Where will you be driving it most often?" My answer would define HOW THE BENEFITS OF THE CAR SPECIFICALLY APPLIED TO ME. A perfect application of The Benefit of The Benefit.

I asked the young man (also named Steve) where he had studied sales. He said he'd been with the dealership since graduating from high school a few years ago. He read a lot of sales books and took several seminars, all on his own (and all tax deductible). That was it, a self-made salesperson. I was standing before a natural.

I answered his question, stating, "I'll be taking some fairly long trips as well as just driving a few miles to work each day."

"Great choice," he replied. "The larger six cylinder engine will give you the power you'll need on the open road, but still give you pretty good mileage for your shorter runs. The larger leather bucket seats along with the cruise control will make those long hauls a lot nicer. And it's a very classy car. I've got the keys right here. Why don't you take it out and see if it fits." He handed me the keys. "Let me know what you think."

When I got back, I was in automotive love. This was *the* car. I tried not to look too anxious, hoping to strike as good a deal as possible.

"I don't know about you, but I really hate the haggling that goes on in most car dealers," he said as I told him I'd like to strike a deal on the car. "You saw the sticker price, why don't you make me an offer and I'll see if the manager gives it a thumbs up."

For a moment, I flinched. Here it was. Good cop, bad cop. I tensed, awaiting the endless offer, counteroffer nonsense that this guy just said he hated as much as I. I made what I thought was a fair offer, low, but fair. He left, only to reappear in less than two minutes (digital watch).

"Mr. Bryant, we have a deal," he said. "You'll be able to drive your new car off the lot in about an hour."

I was stunned. When all the necessary paperwork was finished, I asked him why he didn't try to get a little more money out of the sale.

"Mr. Bryant, you told me about your busy life," (I had alluded to QVC and other endeavors, realizing I had done so while responding to what appeared to be his innocent questions). "I figured if we didn't strike a deal right away, you'd walk. Your offer was a little low, but we still made money and gained a new customer. I figure we both won."

He was right. I really enjoy the new car and when it's time for another, I'll be back, as long as he's still there. Of course with chutzpa like that, he might own his own dealership by then. And Iacocca has announced his retirement.

"WHERE WILL YOU BE DRIVING IT MOST OFTEN?"...Sometimes, The Benefit of The Benefit is as simple as that.

Benefit of The Benefit — Summary

Simply stated, The Benefit of The Benefit is exactly how the benefits of a product and/or service specifically apply to your customer. To define it, you must first go through the exercise of finding the general benefit(s) of a product.

The sales process usually establishes a product's *features, advantages and benefits.*

To find a *feature* of a product, fill in the blank in the statement "This is _____."

An *advantage* can be identified by completing the statement "Which does _____."

A general *benefit* for a product can be defined by "Which means _____."

A *Benefit of The Benefit* can then be identified by expanding on the last statement by adding "Which means _____ to my customer.

Recall the story of Charlie, the traditional copier salesperson who took the time to identify the benefits of his product to a major segment of his customers, the automotive aftermarket. He did this by first understanding their sales problems. Once he established that most of their profitability came from servicing private and municipal fleets, and that these sales were *extremely* price sensitive, we set out to find a way to make his product the answer for this problem.

We proposed that these automotive aftermarket dealers create a newsletter for their fleet customers. This document would provide their customers with service information as well as some money saving tips and promotional offers. Since they would need powerful, advanced copiers to create this newsletter, Charlie's company stood to gain a great deal of business from this idea.

The general benefit of owning a better copier was improved communication between the automotive aftermarket companies and their fleet customers. The Benefit of The Benefit became LOSING LESS BUSINESS DUE TO PRICE. Sometimes identifying and utilizing The Benefit of The Benefit can be a lot of work, but in the highly competitive 1990's (and beyond), it's a real necessity.

In the world of sales, we are all inclined to ease off when times are good. When your product is selling very well, there is a tendency to let the "if it ain't broke, don't fix it" philosophy take over. I say, that's exactly when you should increase your efforts. If you wait until things are bad to step up your sales and marketing thrust, you already have a negative to counteract before you start to sell.

Earlier, I noted the time when I sold a line of skin care products on QVC. The product had historically done very well. Most other hosts who presented it simply did a very polished features, advantages, benefits presentation. It always worked, so the feeling was "why rock the boat."

I did some personal research and brainstorming and hit upon several common situations where skin care would be the most necessary. When a random caller told me she spent a great deal of time in her car (where, I had discovered, the air was extremely dry and damaging) I had an opportunity to unleash a

Benefit of The Benefit: HOW MUCH BETTER YOU WOULD FEEL AND YOUR SKIN WOULD LOOK AFTER USING THE PRODUCT TO COUNTERACT THE ADVERSE CONDITIONS THAT EXIST IN A COMMON SITUATION.

As soon as I hit upon this fact, sales for the product increased dramatically. Although you might not be able to track your progress as immediately as we can with direct television selling, your efforts at defining Benefits of The Benefits will increase your sales.

Using your own product can be another effective way to identify The Benefit of The Benefit. How many times have you seen a hair stylist whose own coif looked like a cross between Don King's distinctive locks and Phyllis Diller's wild "do?" Did their unkempt appearance inspire confidence in their ability? If you're like me, you want the person cutting your hair to be as well groomed (at all times) as you hope to be after they're finished with you.

I can't tell you how many times I've had to face a clothing salesperson who looked as if he or she were one step away from living on the streets. Nothing I'd rather do than buy a good suit from someone wearing cheap, threadbare polyester. I'm really going to take their fashion advice seriously...about as seriously as I do the average Daffy Duck cartoon. And you're probably nodding in recognition because you've experienced the same thing time and time again.

Although the disheveled hair cutter and frumpy clothing salesperson should be responsible for their own appearance, I lay the lion's share of the blame with their employers. Think about all the "messy" salespeople you've refused to deal with and multiply that times the over two hundred and fifty million people living in this country. The amount of lost sales is staggering. (Owners of beauty salons and clothing stores take note!)

In my own case, using a product that I was selling is best typified by my experiences selling a weight loss plan on QVC. Even though most of the plan's success stories came from people who had massive amounts of weight to lose, I decided to try it to lose just 20 pounds.

I used my personal testimonial to establish HOW GOOD I FELT AND LOOKED AFTER LOSING ONLY 20 POUNDS BY USING THE PLAN as a new Benefit of The Benefit for the plan. This new angle, discovered through my personal use of the plan, brought in a tremendous number of new customers — customers who thought the plan would only work if you were severely overweight.

I'm not saying that I wouldn't have hit upon this very Benefit of The Benefit without using the product myself, but it was certainly easier this way. And I had the power of a personal testimonial to back up the new claim.

Providing better customer service both before and after the sale is another excellent way to establish how the general benefits of your product specifically apply to your customers (thereby identifying The Benefits of The Benefits). This is especially true with "service-before-the-sale." The easier you make it for your customers to buy your product, the more likely *they* are to listen and participate in your sales presentation. Active listening and participation on their part will make it much easier for you to identify additional Benefits of the Benefits of your product.

Take a moment and think about how many times you've walked out of a store without buying something you wanted or needed because you couldn't find an open cash register. We've all done that too many times (and stores like Macy's are wondering why they're filing for Chapter 11 protection).

The same factors apply in any sales situation. If it's difficult for your customer to order, pay for, or get delivery on your product, you probably won't get the sale.

I cited the example of John, the young clothing salesman who went what some might consider to be "overboard" to service his customers. Yet in going out of his way to service a customer, he was able to identify an extremely effective Benefit of The Benefit of his product for future sales situations: HAVING ALL THE BENEFITS OF A NEW WARDROBE WITHOUT HAVING TO MAKE REPEATED TRIPS TO THE STORE.

John learned several new skills (alterations, color consultation, style fads versus trends etc.) which enabled him to sell an entire seasonal wardrobe to a busy executive *on the telephone*. John's extra efforts catapulted him into a successful career. Yours can do the same for you.

The specific benefits of your product or service will be different for each specific group of customers. Take the example of when my advertising agency was asked to help sell a computer software system that saved both time and money for the end user. One general benefit of the system was a better bottom line for the company using it. This made one Benefit of The Benefit to the decision maker (a company executive) a recapitulation of the general benefit itself, SAVING TIME AND MONEY. We devised a media presentation to market the software that saved the executive a great deal of time and money compared to conventional sales presentations. This created a truly textbook example of The Benefit of The Benefit.

However, if the decision maker had been a computer programmer, then unless he or she had some type of "piecework" arrangement, The Benefit of The Benefit would have been very different than that for a company principal. If the programmer was a salaried employee, then The Benefit of The Benefit (if you're defining the general benefit as a better bottom line) would be THE POSSIBILITY OF A BETTER TOTAL COMPENSATION PACKAGE GENERATED FROM THE COMPANY'S IMPROVED PROFITABILITY.

If the programmer (and decision maker) were a freelance employee, a general benefit of this software system would be more time for other projects. This would make The Benefit of The Benefit A BETTER PERSONAL BOTTOM LINE BY USING THE TIME SAVED FOR OTHER MONEY MAKING PROJECTS. The Benefit of The Benefit is different in almost every instance. Sometimes it changes for every person. Other times, it can apply to a specific group, but *it is always in flux.*

A complete knowledge of the product you are selling is crucial to properly identifying The Benefit of The Benefit. Colleges and university professors are *wonderful* sources of information. Establishing a network of experts is one of the most effective things you can do to become a better salesperson.

Computer databases (Compuserve, Prodigy, etc.) are also excellent research sources along with main branches of major metropolitan libraries.

You have already read about Sara, the retail electronics salesperson who used her product knowledge as a powerful "listening tool." She would listen to her customers' needs and use her better-than-average knowledge to match them to the right equipment. Although this seems like it should be obvious to even the most neophyte of salespeople, many use their knowledge to "show off" their superiority.

These know-it-all salespeople may be authority figures, but they always come off holier-than-thou. They make recommendations based on their understanding of their products with little or no regard to their customers (if in fact they have any).

Sara used her knowledge to make her customers feel like they played an important part in the sales process (and they did). By USING HER KNOWL-EDGE TO FIND OUT HOW THE GENERAL BENEFITS OF THE AVAILABLE UNITS WOULD SPECIFICALLY APPLY TO HER CUSTOMERS, Sara became a sales success. Learn all you can about your product and then listen to your customer!

Finally, sometimes, The Benefit of The Benefit can be defined in *one* simple question. The "Where will you be driving it most often?" query detailed a few pages back is an excellent example of this. Too many salespeople waste valuable time going through a litany of interrogatories trying to define a simple benefit. Don't get lost in the process. Just like good magic, good sales are simple and direct!

Section 2: Prospecting with The Benefit of The Benefit

Prospecting

Whether you are involved in retail or corporate sales, prospecting is vital to your success (although many retail sales people don't realize this). Without a constant supply of new leads, your customer universe will not support a growing income. While an entire book could be written on just this subject (and many good ones already have), there are a few important points to consider when prospecting with The Benefits of The Benefits of your product.

However, before I get to any specific techniques, it's important to realize that prospecting is just that — *prospecting*! It is not selling! The entire object of prospecting is to get a face-to-face meeting with a prospective customer. Except for magazine subscriptions, time shares and various contest scams, very few products or services are sold while prospecting.

Identifying The Benefits of The Benefits for your product while prospecting will open more doors than other more conventional approaches. Try these:

Prospecting Idea #1 — Cold Calls

I probably hate cold calls more than you do. They used to make me shiver, break out in a sweat, raise my voice a full octave and generally make me think I was slime. Pretty bad, right? However, once I learned how to apply The Benefit of The Benefit to cold calling, I relaxed. I still didn't love it, but at least I was successful at it. Whether calling someone about the advertising agency I worked for or simply trying to book myself as a magician, by using The Benefit of The Benefit, my cold calls were getting results.

The first thing to understand about cold call prospecting is that once someone says he or she is not interested in your product, you are no longer talking to a *prospect*. No amount of salesmanship (or even begging) will change his or her mind. When someone expresses no interest in what you're selling, especially after you've identified how your product specifically benefits him or her, say "thank you," followed by "goodbye" and hang up the phone. Better to use your time on someone who shows some interest.

Call early! Most cold-callers usually wait until after 9:00 AM to start calling, thinking that most people won't be receptive to their ideas until that time. Wrong! Most successful people start their day well before 9:00 AM, often before 8:00. Try calling at 8:00 or even before. The worst that could happen is that a security guard will tell you that nobody is there yet. But if your prospect *is* there, chances are that he or she will answer the phone in person, without the assistance of a Phone Troll who usually won't arrive until 9:00.

When you make a cold call after 9:00, you will most likely have to deal with some kind of Phone Troll. This could be the phone operator, secretary or assistant. It is his or her job to screen the calls for your prospect — don't get angry with them for doing their job. Just like in the days of old, the consequences of making a Troll angry are extremely unpleasant.

To get past this first hurdle of cold calling, I've found it best to identify yourself and your company and then ask to speak with your prospect. Speak slowly and pleasantly. If the Phone Troll questions you, simply repeat your name, company and ask to speak with your prospect again. This "broken record" technique will usually do the trick.

Should the person ask, "What does this concern?" be upfront and mention The Benefit of the Benefit you were going to use with your prospect. Something like "Yes, my company has a product that will help Mr. Bryant write his next book in half the time it took to write the last one. May I speak with him please?" (If you can't get through to me with a specific benefit like that, I've got to get a new Phone Troll.)

If you are told, "Mr. Bryant wouldn't be interested," or something in a similar vein, stop pitching then and there. Don't antagonize the person on the phone. It's most effective to say something like "I understand that Mr. Bryant is very busy. Simply tell him that John Smith from XYZ Corporation called concerning a product that will help him write his next book in half the time. I can be reached at 555-5555. Just ask for John Smith. Of course, XYZ's number is in the book. I hope to hear from him soon." You'd be surprised at how many times simply asking for a callback after stating a specific benefit has worked for me. Many times the prospect called me the same day.

Nancylee, a Director for the Mary Kay Cosmetics Company, has an extremely innovative method for dealing with Phone Trolls. She makes several cold calls to major corporations each year, trying to sell them on the idea of using Mary Kay products as staff and customer Christmas gifts. When she is asked "What's this in reference to?" she replies, "I hope this doesn't spoil the surprise, but it's about a gift for you."

Her unique approach has gotten her through the Phone Troll every time! You might be able to adapt her methodology to fit your product or service. For example, if you are selling office equipment, try countering a "What's this in reference to?" question with something like "I hope this isn't letting the cat out of the bag, but it's about getting you some help with that heavy workload of yours." Again, if you get a "we're not interested," after trying a technique like this, say "thank you, goodbye," and go in search of a *real* prospect.

Once you do get beyond the Phone Troll, identify yourself and your company again and then ask the prospect if he or she would be interested in _____ (a specific benefit of your product). Something like "Mr. Bryant, would you like to be able to write your next book in half the time it took you to write the last one?" (If you have a product like this, call my publisher!!!)

See what I mean? The salesperson has already told the prospect that he or she understands the prospect's business and that they have a product or service that will help. Go into any cold call with this kind of information and your success rate will improve. Just be "locked and loaded" with as many specific benefits as possible before making your call.

If the prospect is interested, your next move is to make the appointment. Never say "I can see you anytime that's convenient for you." That sounds like you are really unsuccessful. I've found it best to give the prospect two choices, like "Great, I can meet with you at 3:00 PM Monday or 4:45 on Thursday this week." If neither time is good, go to the next week and give three options. That will usually do the trick.

Remember, the busier you sound, the more successful you sound. And successful people want to deal with successful people.

Prospecting Idea #2 — Media Prospecting

Articles and stories in magazines, newspapers, or on radio and TV have traditionally been great sources for prospecting information. A salesperson would see a story about someone who needs their product and then attempt to use that information as an introduction. The salesperson would either write to or call the person to congratulate them and then hope to use this foot-in-the-door to make a sale.

This is a "reactive numbers game." (The more people you contact, the more chances you have of selling.) If you identify your product's benefits as they apply to a publicized individual, you create a "proactive, targeted sales presentation." (I love words like that.)

For example, let's say you're a sales person at a camera store. To increase your sales, simply read the birth announcements in the newspaper every day. Call the new parents to tell them you have just the right "auto-everything" camera to capture their new heir on film. If their phone number is unlisted, use the address information in the article and send them some information on your easiest and best cameras. You have identified a specific benefit of your product that applies to new parents — namely PRESERVING THE CHILDHOOD OF THEIR OFFSPRING WITH A GOOF-PROOF CAMERA THAT TAKES GREAT PHOTOS EVERY TIME.

Make sure you also include a compelling reason for the person to purchase the product from you to receive this specific benefit. Some sort of sale, limited-time offer or gift with purchase are excellent motivators.

Is this too much work for a retail salesperson? Not for one who wants to succeed. This one proactive step will set you aside from at least 95% of your peers.

A corporate or one-on-one salesperson could use the same strategy. Just scan a publication (newspapers are the most immediate) for a story about someone who needs your product. As you are reading, keep asking the question, "How could my _____ specifically benefit this person?" As soon as you have an answer, you have identified a specific benefit and you're ready to make your prospecting pitch.

Again, a compelling reason to buy *now* and *from you* should be part of your presentation. Like the retail scenario above, some kind of limited-time savings or other "no-cost" add-on will greatly help your efforts. Just be certain to use this information as a way to get the face-to-face meeting with your prospect. Sell the appointment on the phone, sell your product in person!

Prospecting Idea #3 — Referrals

Most good salespeople will ask a satisfied customer if he or she knows anyone else who could use their product. However, if you have already identified how the benefit(s) of your product specifically apply to a customer, why not ask if they know someone else who would enjoy the same Benefit of The Benefit of your product. Asking for referrals like this will result in a lot more *valid* sales leads, since the people being referred not only need your product, but (according to your customer) also need one or more of its specific benefits.

When speaking to a referred prospect, make sure you immediately say who recommended that you call. You'd be surprised at how many salespeople handle this type of prospecting like a common cold call, with no mention of the referral whatsoever. A familiar name spoken at the beginning of your presentation will open more doors than just about any other prospecting technique.

Prospecting Idea #4 — Newsletters

An informational newsletter about your product is a very powerful prospecting tool. Include success stories about people who are enjoying specific benefits of your product as well as tips and general information about the product and your target market. It doesn't have to be a major publication; a few pages is fine. Publish it regularly; monthly is fine as long as you can maintain that kind of publication schedule. If not, put it out bi-monthly. Make sure you stick to the publication schedule.

Just like the newsletter used by Charlie, the copier salesperson mentioned earlier in this text, your newsletter should be sent to current customers as well as prospects. A little freebie like this is an excellent prospecting tool for new *and* existing customers alike.

Prospecting Idea #5 — Visibility Prospecting

Anything you can do to get your product in the public eye is Visibility Prospecting. The more people who see it, the more chances you have of reaching a prospect. And there are some great ways to get this visibility without spending a dime.

Become an expert! Actually, you should already be an expert about your product or service. Write letters to the local newspapers as well as the news and public affairs departments of radio and TV stations. Let reporters and editors know about your expertise and that you would be willing to be a spokesperson in any article or on any show or report that would require your expertise.

When you set yourself up as an expert in any field, first make sure you can answer any question within the realm of your expertise. Flub a question or get a fact wrong and simply kiss your "expert" status good-bye. Also, be ready to be contacted at all hours of the day or night. That's a small price to pay for the exposure.

I used Expert Prospecting in my career as a magician. I let the local media know that I was available to share my know-how anytime they needed me. I was featured on over a dozen news reports within a year along with quotes (and photos) in many newspaper articles. This visibility led to several bookings.

Volunteer your time. If there's a charity that involves a great number of your prospects...volunteer! For example, if you're selling medical equipment, volunteer your time at a hospital or rehabilitation facility.

Don't try to sell while you're volunteering, that would be as transparent as glass. Use this visibility to your advantage in future cold calls and selling situations. And don't feel guilty about it, you're providing a much needed volunteer service. Just make sure you're serious about making the commitment to volunteer on a regular basis. Almost as bad as trying to sell while you're volunteering is showing up only when you feel like it or when someone you want to impress is going to be there.

Summary

Prospecting is the life's blood of any sales job. Showing your customers that you know enough about their business to identify how your product *specifically* benefits them will maximize your prospecting efforts.

When making cold calls, call early, well before 9:00 AM. Not only are people more receptive to new ideas at this time, they will also be more likely to answer their own phone. If the prospect is not interested in what you are selling, thank the person, say goodbye and hang up the phone. A person who is not interested is really not a prospect.

If the prospect is interested, don't try to sell your product on the telephone. The purpose of the prospecting call is to get a face-to-face meeting with the prospect. Any actual selling is more effectively done in person.

If an operator, secretary or assistant answers the phone, identify yourself, your company and ask to speak to the prospect. If you are questioned, try repeating the same information. If this doesn't work, try to intrigue the person by making it sound important that the prospect call you back as soon as possible. You could also act like you'd be spoiling a surprise by supplying any additional information. If you still cannot get through, don't waste your time, go in search of another *valid* prospect.

Search the media (newspapers, magazines, radio and TV) for articles about people who sound like they could benefit from using your product. If possible, call them and explain how the benefits of your product specifically apply to them. Again, sell the appointment on the phone, sell your product in person.

Whenever possible, ask existing customers if they know of anyone who could use the same benefits of the product that they are enjoying. When you contact a referred customer, use the name of the referring customer as soon as possible to add credibility to your presentation.

A regularly published informational newsletter is also an excellent prospecting tool. Include general information about your product or service as well case histories about your customers. Mail the newsletter to prospects and existing customers.

Offering your product expertise to local TV and radio stations as well as newspapers is a form of Visibility Prospecting. Once people in your area come to recognize you as an expert, they will view you as *the* person to deal with for your particular product.

You can also volunteer your time to organizations who have some kind of tie-in with your product. Don't sell while volunteering, simply use the visibility and relationships you develop to help in your future prospecting efforts.

Effective prospecting is no illusion. In fact, the results can be downright magical.

Section 3: Closing with The Benefit of The Benefit

Closing Techniques: Close The Sale, Not The Door

I love sales books. There are some wonderful works on the bookshelves today. If you're as voracious a reader as I, then you've probably noticed there's also an almost equal number of really bad sales books out there as well.

Most truly bad sales books that I've read stress "closing techniques." And they have hundreds of "proven power closes." Perhaps the most used (and my least favorite) is the Ben Franklin close. You have to love this one.

You are supposed to use the Ben Franklin close when your customer is trying to talk him or herself out of buying your product. To counteract this, you are supposed to say something like, "You know, I was reading about Ben Franklin the other day. (Sure, we all read about our founding fathers on a daily basis, don't we?) I read that whenever he had a tough decision to make, he would take a sheet of paper and draw a line down the middle of it (arts and crafts, I'm loving this more all the time). Then he would list all the positives of the decision on one side of the paper and all the negatives on the other (Ben obviously had a great deal of time on his hands.)

"Then, Ben would make his decision based on which was greater — the negatives or the positives. So, Mr. Customer, let's take a sheet of paper and I'll help you list the positives and negatives of my product. Let's see if the positives outweigh the negatives."

If you encounter anyone, a corporate executive, retail customer...*ANYONE* who falls for this strategy, go for the jugular. Obviously, P.T. Barnum was right! In fact, with today's larger population, maybe there's one born every half-minute.

Conventional sales wisdom says that to arrive at the point where you should begin closing a sale, you must establish three factors: trust, need and value. I believe that by first defining The Benefits of The Benefits of your product, you combine these three factors in a very logical manner.

> 1. *Trust* — Your customer has to trust you before he or she can make an informed sales decision. The features, advantages, benefits, Benefits of The Benefits process allows

you to establish trust by using an informed approach to discover exactly how the benefit(s) of your product or service apply to your customer.

2. *Need* — Likewise, by showing your customer how his or her specific needs are met by your product, you are stressing *need* right from the start of the sales process.

3. *Value* — The Benefits of the Benefits have the value of your product built-in to their very precepts.

Using this strategy, you are presenting a "united front" of trust, need and value to your customer. Instead of establishing separate "beachheads" for each individual factor, you are simplifying the process for everyone concerned.

So what about all the stories we've heard about those great sales presentations where the salesperson covered all the bases, had the customer virtually eating out of his or her hand and left without getting the order? Proponents of using a closing technique as a separate part of the sales process would say, "Aha! The salesperson didn't ask for the order."

I'm *not* saying that there isn't a time to "cut to the chase" and ask for the order, but I am stressing that this process must be an integral component of your entire sales presentation. If you put on the brakes to find the close, your customer is going to stop right along with you. All the trust, need and value you've established will vaporize as your customer realizes that it's time to write the check.

Rather than shoot off a flare signaling the end of communication (which is what a separate close can do), I suggest some soft-edged questions to determine whether you've established The Benefits of The Benefits to your customer. Something like this:

"How do you feel this _____ meets your needs?" If the response is positive, then ask for the order with a question like: "Would you like delivery on Tuesday or Thursday?" In a situation where delivery isn't a factor, ask a similar action question like, "Would you like some help to get this to your car?" or perhaps an upsell type of question, such as "Do you prefer solid or striped shirts with a style like this?"

If you get a negative response to the question "How do you feel this _____ meets your needs?" then use your product and customer knowledge to explore and defuse the objection. In this instance, a follow-up question like "How important is (the point raised as an objection) to (you, your family, your company)?" Based on this answer, you will know whether your product is a proper match for your client. If not, move to another product that's a closer match to your customer's needs.

If you don't have a product that meets (or preferably exceeds) the needs your customer feels to be important, then stop the sale. Sure, there are many ways to force a square peg into a round hole. I've read many books that tell you to "make the sale no matter what!" Great for meeting your the end-of-the-month quota, but lousy in the big picture.

I know a salesman (Bob) who used to sell big ticket phone systems to major corporations. He was fresh out of college, eager to show that his drive and ability would take him right to the top. He was good at making his products sound like the be-all and end-all in telecommunications systems. Whatever your needs, his system met them today and would continue to do so for an infinite time in the future.

His timing was great, since he entered the field right after AT&T was broken up by the federal government. Corporations who had relied on the communications giant for all their telecommunications needs were now faced with an almost endless array of possibilities from large and small equipment manufacturers. Bob worked for one of the Johnny-Come-Lately companies.

His telecommunications systems were much less expensive than those offered by AT&T and most of their competitors. And, on paper and in his pitch, they sounded like the best possible value. Unfortunately, they were woefully inadequate for companies that had a heavy volume of incoming calls.

For a few years after the AT&T divestiture, most corporate decision makers were not informed enough to make non-AT&T equipment decisions. After all, Western Electric (AT&T's equipment division) had met their needs for decades. It used to be as simple as just placing the order. Now they had some serious catching up to do.

Enter Bob — glib, knowledgeable and a fine *traditional* salesperson. Unfortunately, he was just what they didn't need.

Bob was a "killer" for his first year; his company's top producer. He seemed destined for greatness until the systems he sold began to fail...miserably! (Can you say "crash and burn?" I knew you could.)

Bob's customers became extremely familiar with the service and repair division of his company. As system after system failed, Bob's customers began to initiate lawsuits against his company (lost business, breach of good faith, etc.). Soon, Bob's company had dozens of court battles on their hands. Even the customers who weren't having problems began to dump their systems to avoid any future failures.

Bob went from being his company's number one salesperson to unemployed in less than two years. (I don't know what ever happened to Bob, but I've heard rumors that he went into politics.)

I know this is an extreme example, but realize, if you close a sale for a product or service that you know won't meet your customer's needs, you'll have problems hanging on you like a cheap suit.

A Magical Interlude

Harry Anderson, the star of NBC's *Night Court* and a very accomplished magician, started his professional life as a con man. Really! Harry would often drink "free" at a bar all evening by winning several "can't lose" bets.

One of his favorite scams was covering a full glass with his hat and betting the unwary spectators that he could drain the glass dry without touching or in any way disturbing the hat. As soon as they accepted the wager, he would then bend down and pretend to drain the glass dry. He would then claim that the glass was empty and urge the patrons to pay up.

Although they would repeatedly doubt his word, he held fast to his claim that the glass was empty. Finally, in an attempt to prove him wrong, one of the neophyte gamblers would lift up the hat to show the glass was full...which it always was. Then, Harry would pick up the glass and drink it dry, *without touching his hat.* At this point, the spectators usually paid him. Unfortunately, there was that one time when a disgruntled loser broke his jaw. With the hundreds of times that Harry won that bet, I'd wager all his winnings that he remembers that "loss" much more vividly than all the "wins."

Back to some additional closing techniques. Again, I feel strongly that your close should be woven throughout any sales presentation. I know I'm flying in the face of tradition here, since most of the sales superstars of the 70's and 80's segregated the close as a separate element. It worked and worked well...for those times. Retail and corporate customers have become more sophisticated in the 1990's. Their knowledge of consumer affairs and sales in general makes them very tough customers.

Once these savvy customers know you're going for the close, they'll shut down like one of Bob's overloaded telecommunications systems. And when they've turned off, the sale stops then and there. You might be able to reinterest them at another time, but your current battle is over.

There are quite a few ways to use The Benefit of The Benefit to begin closing as soon as you begin the sale. Most of them fall along the lines of what has been traditionally called *The Assumptive Close*, which, as the name implies, *assumes* your customer is buying your product. Here are some examples of *assumptive* questions:

Corporate Closing Questions:

"How does this _____ fit into your growth plans?" (Although you should have already shown exactly how your product will do this, it's very productive to get your customer's response as well. If the customer simply recapitulates what you've said, you're right on track. Should he or she come up with some aspects that you neglected, use your product/customer knowledge to hone in on some "new and improved" Benefits of The Benefits.)

"What would be your alternative to _____?" (This will identify your competition and allow you to sharpen the focus of The Benefits of The Benefits for your product.)

"Can you see any reasons why this _____ won't meet your needs?" (As this is essentially a negative question, use it sparingly. I use it most often to begin a dialogue with an unresponsive customer.)

"Where would be the best place to put this _____?" (A soft-edged assumption. You've already assumed that your customer has bought. Conventional sales wisdom would make this "assumptive close" a separate part of the sales process. If you have shown your customer The Benefits of The Benefits for your product throughout your presentation, this "close" becomes a logical extension of the sale. When your customer answers, he or she will be in a benefits-oriented mode. Their answer will most likely reflect the location that will provide the most specific benefits to their company. By now, you'll be able to "kill" with that kind of additional information.)

"Who will be using this _____ most often?" (Identifying the user can allow you to target even more specific Benefits of The Benefits. In this instance, you must have a thorough understanding of your customer's day-to-day operations to make the best use of the information provided by the answer to this question.)

If you haven't noticed by now, most *assumptive* questions conform to the old "who, what, where, when, why and how" questions that every journalist tries to answer. The goal is the same in the world of corporate and retail sales, although the questions are obviously different for both fields.

Retail Closing Questions:

"Where (and/or when) will you be (driving, wearing, using, etc.) _____ most often?" (As stated earlier in this book, this is probably my favorite question in the world of retail sales. It cuts through the fog and literally makes the customer tell you exactly how the benefits of the product apply to him or her.)

"How will _____ work with the rest of your (clothing or jewelry wardrobe, your home entertainment center, kitchen appliances, etc.)?" (A great lifestyle question that should identify at least one Benefit of The Benefit for your product.)

"What do you hope to achieve by using _____?" (Asking goal-oriented questions is a great way to have your customer "mentally amortize" the cost of your product over a course of years. Obviously, this is a question better asked for a self-improvement product like exercise equipment rather than a refrigerator.)

"Why do you prefer this model, style, pattern, color, etc.) of _____?" (Allowing the customer to "sell" him or herself on your product is a fine way to identify additional Benefits of The Benefits. A customer's answer to this question should also provide you with useful information for add-on sales.)

"Who else in your family will be using _____?" (Identifying additional users can help to target even more Benefits of The Benefits for your product.)

Keep in mind that there are an infinite number of questions that will help you to make an *assumptive* close throughout the sales process in a Benefits of The Benefits-type presentation. It's a good idea to devote some time each day to coming up with one or more new questions.

However, as important as these closing-related questions are, keep in mind that they can be overused. This is especially true when your customer has already made the decision to buy. Many sales are lost through overselling. Check out the following example:

While shopping for a new home with a realtor, I found a great place. Wonderful layout, super location, excellent price. I spent several more minutes walking through the house and around the grounds than I had with any other property. This should have been a flare to the realtor. Stop, do not pass go, *do* collect sales commission. My "buying signal" was there. All this guy had to do was look and *listen* for it.

You know what's coming next, don't you?

After spending at least twice as much time perusing this place as I had with all the others, he announced "We still have four more places to see before dark, Steve. We'd better get moving."

He blew it! I went from ready-to-buy back to anticipation of what the next properties might look like. We made it to all four before dark and then went back to his office. "Well, what did you think?" he asked.

"I'm not sure," I replied. "I'd like to take all the spec sheets home and give it some thought."

He agreed and let me walk out the door (a wise move since I was really overwhelmed by the choices I had seen). I went home and gave it some thought. Although I was in a position to buy a new home (especially the one that had made such an initial impression), I was really struck by the opulance of the last house we saw. It was at the top end of my affordability range, costing a great deal more than my earlier "dream house," but it was great! A swimming pool, sauna, finished basement...the whole house reeked of success.

Even though this literal palace didn't feel as much like home as the place I had seen earlier, all my programming said this expensive place was where a successful person should live — even if the mortgage payments would leave me more than a little land poor. Still, I talked myself out of the more humble abode and set about the task of finding out whether I could really afford the more elegant house.

I couldn't, at least not yet. When the realtor called, I told him that I was going to wait and see if I could juggle or increase my finances to afford the bigger place. I couldn't.

He called a few more times but my financial situation remained unchanged and I eventually talked myself out of moving for a while.

It wasn't until years later that I realized I would have been very happy with the smaller house he had shown if I hadn't seen the "killer house." This realtor oversold me. When I was so impressed with that one property, he should have taken me back to the office then and there and started the paperwork.

Unfortunately, like many salespeople, he had one way of doing things. He had set up seven appointments that day and come hell or high water, we were going to see them all. Think of the times something similar has happened to you. You're all ready to buy and then the salesperson gives you too many options. Overkill!

When you're giving a Benefits of The Benefits presentation and your customer is obviously impressed enough to buy well before you've finished what you planned to say, STOP! Cut the deal, make the sale! If the customer closes the sale for you, be attentive enough, *listen closely enough* to get the message.

Sell your customer what he or she wants, when they want to buy it. That may be the most powerful closing technique of them all.

Closing Summary

Using The Benefits of The Benefits approach to sales allows you to close at all times during your sales presentation. Since you are showing your customer how the benefits of your product apply to him or her throughout your presentation, you are repeatedly giving them the opportunity to say "YES."

The accepted sales factors of *Trust, Need and Value* are presented as a unified element when your presentation is based on the specific benefits your customer will receive from your product. There is no need to segregate your close from the rest of your presentation. You will find it is literally "built-in."

The Assumptive Close — assuming that your customer is buying your product — is the easiest of those "built-in" closes to use in a Benefits of The Benefits presentation. Since you are showing your customer the specific benefits he or she will receive from your product throughout your sales presentation, it is logical to *assume* that they are buying.

Asking questions about "who, what, where, when and why" your product will be used will facilitate this *assumptive* type of close. These types of questions make your customer think of even more specific benefits of your product, strengthening the *assumption* that he or she is going to buy.

If you find out that your product doesn't meet the needs of your customer, STOP THE SALE. Any immediate gain you have from closing the sale on a product that won't do the job for your customer will never be worth all the bad publicity (and possible lawsuits).

Watch and (especially) listen for your customer's buying signals. If your customer finds the right product after only a few minutes of your planned presentation, MAKE THE SALE. Too often salespeople get stuck in a "that's the way I've always done it" rut. Trying to get to all their carefully planned points, they often miss the fact that their customer was ready to say yes several minutes earlier. Overselling your product like this can confuse your customer, causing him or her to delay or even cancel their buying decision.

Just as the finale of a magic trick is the payoff to the whole process, the close is the culmination of any sales effort. And like an illusion, if you learn all the steps leading up to the climax, a successful ending is assured.

Section 4: Selling with the Written Word

Change-ups, Curves & other Written Pitches

All too often, the written proposal or sales letter is the sole property of the corporate salesperson. I feel that a Benefits of The Benefits-oriented sales proposal or letter can work effectively in almost any sales situation, whether it's corporate or retail. In this section, you will learn how to apply the techniques you've learned in this book to writing powerful sales letters or proposals for any selling circumstance.

Probably some of the finest examples of selling with the written word are in your mailbox right now — direct mail. (You might refer to it as junk mail, but it generates billions of dollars of revenue each year. That's my kind of junk!)

Writers of effective direct mail copy realize they only have a few seconds to grab your attention before their written pitch hits the circular file. So what do they lead off with? Right: Benefits! They make the benefits as specific as possible for their huge audience. (Sometimes the same mailing will go to tens of millions of homes.) Sound familiar? Yes, they are going for The Benefits of The Benefits whenever possible and they do it right in the opening line of the letter.

Phrases like "How would you like to spend the rest of your life lying on the beach in front of your home while everyone else is working long, hard hours just to make ends meet?" Sure, it's trite and hokey (and I'm not suggesting you ever try to copy their writing style), but it works. Whether you're intrigued by a new lifestyle or just curious about what kind of scam it is this time, chances are you continue to read the letter until your curiosity is satisfied. By then, you might just decide to subscribe to *Aardvark Lovers* magazine just to have a chance at The Good Life (or maybe you've always loved aardvarks and no one ever took the time to identify that need).

See what I mean? We've all received laser-printed, "personal" direct mail letters that promise us something great, sometimes even on the envelope itself. Nothing specific about how to receive this benefit, you just know it's there, beckoning to you.

Proposals

I hit upon this fact early because it will help you to understand the most common mistake made in sales proposals. The benefit is most often placed last in the document. Really, it's almost accepted practice to use the benefit of a sales proposal as the carrot at the end of the stick. Here's an outline of the typical sales proposal.

1. **SCOPE OF PROPOSAL:** In this section, proposal writers detail exactly which products and services they're selling to their customers. I have even written for an advertising agency that had a word processing software package that was a do-it-yourself proposal kit. It had all the sections outlined and fleshed out. All you had to do was fill in the company's name and a description of the product. The software then generated a dull, unfocused document that began with the stirring phrase "The scope of this proposal is to provide XYZ Corporation with _____. The benefits of using _____ are fully outlined in a section later in this document."

   Using this software, you could generate dozens of proposals per day. A real numbers game. Get enough proposals out there and you had to succeed. Guess who didn't use the software? Good answer.

2. **TREATMENT (or) IMPLEMENTATION:** This part of the document describes exactly how the SCOPE will be accomplished. No benefits yet, but the customer knows what he or she is getting (if they haven't fallen asleep by this time).

3. **DELIVERY AND TERMS:** Not a benefit (let alone a Benefit of The Benefit) to be

seen yet. No, in this section you tell the customer when and how much. Some companies even have a section for the customer to initial, indicating that he or she has read this far and agreed to the price (all without knowing how the product will benefit the company).

4. **BENEFITS:** Traditionally placed at the end of a proposal. In the word processing proposal kit I mentioned, this section even had generic benefits already written out — benefits like "XYZ Corporation will experience a gain in productivity, and therefore better profitability by using _____." It sure sold me...on NOT using the software.

I'm sure you're not surprised that I took the time to write individual proposals for customers, making sure I targeted Benefits of The Benefits for each individual customer. I might only be able to write one or two documents a day, but my proposals had better than a 95% acceptance rate. Many times, because I took the time to understand the specific needs of my customers, they would come back to our company for additional services without requesting a proposal.

This is an outline of the proposal document I created, leading off with...

1. **SPECIFIC BENEFITS:** (Since The Benefit of The Benefit is a sales concept, I decided this phraseology would play better to the customer. It did.) Right in the beginning of the document, before the customer even knew exactly what was coming, he or she knew what our product was going to do

for them. I couldn't (and wouldn't) promise them a lifetime of leisure on a tropical beach, but I got their attention by showing them that my company understood their business. We wanted to help and knew how to do it!

2. **TREATMENT (or) IMPLEMENTATION:** Now was the time to tell them what was coming. Even though this was a factual section, I reiterated the benefits and Benefits of The Benefits throughout this part of the proposal.

3. **COST:** Much more direct than DELIVERY AND TERMS. Cut to the chase, here's what it will cost to receive the specific benefits outlined in the above document. If possible, compare the COST with a known expense that has some relationship to your product or service.

4. **DELIVERY OPTIONS:** Since a lot of companies buying advertising services (print pieces, AV and video presentations, catalogs, flyers, press kits) "want them yesterday," I gave them the option of rush delivery along with the cost for a standard turnaround. In the rush delivery section, I borrowed a trick from direct TV marketeers who usually have an express delivery option. I phrased it to let them know how much faster they would be able to enjoy the specific benefits of our products by opting for faster delivery. I never tracked this aspect but I know we had a slew of rush charges while I was with this company

(and we had priced these rush charges to make them excellent profit centers).

5. **SUMMARY:** Since some of the decision makers who would be reading our proposals were extremely busy executives, I included a SUMMARY section. Again, I wove specific benefits throughout this two to four paragraph wrap-up. If this was all he or she read, they were still bombarded with Benefits of The Benefits of our products and/or services.

6. **ACCEPTANCE:** An absolutely essential (and many times overlooked) section for any successful sales proposal. You must give your customer an easy way to say yes. Make sure this section also identifies the person signing as someone who is authorized to make the decision.

Although I've detailed a proposal used in a corporate, big ticket sales situation, there's no reason why the same type of document couldn't be used to sell anything. In retail sales, why not create a simple proposal as a sales tool? Imagine how surprised a retail customer would be to receive a one to four page document highlighting the specific benefits of owning your product.

Don't dismiss this as too much work. I know a shoe salesman who successfully combines marketing concepts with his sales efforts. Here's how he does it:

If someone comes into his store and tries on a few pairs of shoes, Ben will make what appears to be small talk while he is fitting them. What he is actually doing is getting a handle on their lifestyle. Do they stand or walk a great deal in their professional or personal life? Is wearing the latest style important to them or do they have to look "traditionally classic" at work?

From these answers he generates a fact sheet on each customer. Even if they don't buy, he asks for their name and address, telling them that he'll use it to alert them of future sales. Most give the information willingly.

When he mails them a flyer alerting them of latest arrivals, sale prices and so forth, he also includes a small one or two page "formal" proposal, written around their specific needs. Too much time for a simple retail sale? Since most ladies (along with more and more professional men) spend over $2,000 per year on footwear, Ben's efforts at getting the bulk of their business are right on target.

You might ask why he uses the proposal form instead of a more personal letter? Two reasons: First of all, Ben has little background in marketing. He copied the original form of the proposal document he uses from a corporate proposal sent to his store by a supplier (luckily, the document began with a benefits section). Secondly, Ben's store is located in a corporate business park. Since most of his customers are businessmen and women, his proposal is a familiar document to his customers. True, a letter might work just as well, but you can't argue with success.

How successful is he? Well, at 44, he isn't ready for retirement yet and he may not own a 20-room mansion. He does, however, have a nice home as well as two getaway places, one in the mountains and one at the shore. He and his wife drive new Cadillacs every year and his kids go to great colleges. Not bad for a guy who *only* has a high school education.

A Magical Interlude

A young magician was asked by a company to perform at one of their major trade shows. He agreed, even though most of his previous experience consisted of entertaining at small private parties. He was confident that he could put on the type of show the company needed. He proposed a magical extravaganza that would require tens of thousands of dollars in apparatus. The company, impressed with his ability to communicate what he needed along with the specific benefits of every expenditure, agreed to finance the show.

The performance was a hit. The awe-inspiring show attracted more valid sales leads in one hour than the total leads that were generated during the entire run of last year's show. The company, ecstatic at the results, allowed the young performer to keep the expensive equipment, providing he would be available for future shows. The elaborate props allowed the young magical entertainer to move from small private shows to much larger nightclubs and casinos. His career took off like a rocket. David Copperfield would go on to create and perform some of the most unbelievable illusions the world had ever seen.

Sales Letters

Of course, if a full proposal isn't really called for, then a sales letter highlighting specific benefits might be the right thing to do. In a sales letter, you are really creating a mini-proposal, hitting your customer with specific benefits first and then the rest of the details. All of this in a single-page, friendly, effective document.

Again, refer to any well-written (benefits first) direct mail letter. While you aren't promising your customers an early retirement, beginning your sales letter with the specific benefits (The Benefits of The Benefits) for your product, you are increasing the chances of the letter being read in its entirety. The more they read, the more likely they will be to buy.

I'm not suggesting to tell you how to write a dynamite direct mail piece. That's an art form in itself. Although it wouldn't hurt to read a few books on direct mail copywriting, realize that even with their "benefits first" approach, direct marketeers are happy with a one tenth of one percent return rate on their sales packages. They can never make the benefits of their products truly specific in mass mailings that number in the millions. (Still, one tenth of one percent of 50 million is a lot of subscriptions to *Aardvark Lovers* magazine.)

By emulating their approach and taking the time to make the benefits of your product as specific as possible to your customers, your "hit rate" for sales proposals and letters will dwarf theirs.

As an example of how well benefits-laden letters work, take the case of Paul, a magician friend of mine.

I know him because magic, especially sleight-of-hand, has long been an interest of mine. In fact, over a decade ago, I was a trade show magician for some of the largest companies in the country. I wove the benefits of my customers' products into my patter while doing card and coin tricks. Although I no longer have the time to traipse all over the globe proving the hand is more deceptive, not faster, than the eye, I still have a great interest in the magic community.

Paul's skills with a deck of cards and a handful of coins are unreal! He has been a dedicated student of close-up magic since childhood. Yet he had never worked a gig bigger than a local Boy Scout banquet. I asked to see his publicity kit. He had a nice business card and a good looking 8x10 head shot. That was it! And he wondered why he was still working birthday parties.

I asked Paul how he found performing engagements and he told me he was working for many people and groups who had first hired him as a youngster. Many of these people used him to perform at their parties and banquets for more than two decades. He wanted very much to make magic a full-time career, but always had to maintain a second "steady job" to make ends meet.

The first thing I suggested was writing a letter to his existing customers, promising a free performance for every new customer they referred. His party bookings increased by over 200% in a few weeks, more than "paying" for the freebies.

Since Paul had lived in the same town all his life, we drafted another letter to the community's leaders, most of whom knew Paul very well. In this text, we stressed the benefits these people had received from Paul's past performances (improved prestige from more entertaining meetings and parties along with more satisfied constituents for local politicians). The letter went on to stress that Paul's performing abilities and sense of civic pride would make him an excellent spokesperson for the community's efforts to attract new business. No clairvoyance here — most small towns are always trying to increase commerce.

Not only did he get hired as a traveling goodwill ambassador for his community, performing at over two dozen trade fairs per year, but the additional contacts he made at these fairs got him dozens more trade show bookings each year. Since he didn't have any "history" with these new contacts, he made them customers by using brief but formal proposals, tailored to the specific needs of each individual company.

No fancy four-color brochures, touting his uncanny, supernatural, beyond-belief abilities. Just a two or three page proposal, beginning with a SPECIFIC BENEFITS section, mailed along with his 8x10 head shot and business card. (He had lots of both.)

Paul gleaned the individual needs of the companies from sales literature he routinely collected on trade show floors. This homework really paid off. Most companies were accustomed to receiving fancy, showbiz promotional packages from other so-called business-magicians. Paul's focused proposal document showed them that he meant (and understood) business...their business!

He also added a section to the proposal format I had shown him.

Since he was a "seasoned" business performer, having done dozens of shows for his hometown at various trade fairs, he included a REFERENCES section, citing the different trade groups he had worked for in the past.

Paul took the time to make sure that the references he noted were aware he was using their names. Nothing worse than having a prospective customer call someone who doesn't even remember your name, let alone the performance you did for them two years ago. Paul covered all his bases.

Like Ben, Paul isn't a multi-millionaire. He is, however, an extremely happy man since he LOVES what he does for a living — full-time I might add.

Sample Proposal

So that you will have a model of an effective, specific benefits-oriented proposal and sales letter, I'm including the following examples. First, the proposal. This is one our advertising agency used to sell — an ongoing audio newsletter to a major food product manufacturer. The company had created a new salt substitute and wanted to keep its diverse network of independent distributors excited and informed about their product.

A little research showed that most of these independent reps handled over 100 different food products from various manufacturers. While there were few salt substitutes on the market, the product was new and untried. That meant heavy resistance from the buyers for supermarkets and other food chains. Why should a rep waste his or her time trying to sell a new product? Their time would seem to be better spent filling the shelves with the tried and true staples, literally and figuratively the "bread and butter" of these independent distributors.

First, I had to identify the profile of a typical distributor and try to find some common factors. I needed some communal "hooks" to allow me to hang some common benefits. It's always more work than it initially seems.

Remember, I wasn't doing this for a job that was a done deal. In a proposal, you have to create the complete concept for the proposed project with the full realization that this idea might be ripped off. Although this rarely happens, it still infuriates me. If it happens more than once, I simply won't waste my time writing any more proposals for the offending company.

Still, I don't agree with the many advertising and marketing firms who charge for proposals. Even if the proposal cost is deducted in the total cost of the project, I think this is rather bad form. By charging for a proposal, I think you're saying "We don't get that many good ideas, so when one comes along we protect it like the Crown Jewels." Take your chances — you won't get that many lumps.

It took a few hours on the phone to paint the proper picture of the typical sales rep. Although there were many differences between the reps in different parts of the country, there was one *glaring* common factor. You guessed it, the average sales rep spent over half of his or her work time on the road. Drive time! A common factor that allowed me to create a compelling case for an innovative marketing concept: An audio newsletter. Here's how the proposal turned out:

SELLING XYZ SALT SUBSTITUTE THROUGH INDEPENDENT SALES REPS

Specific Benefits

By using the concepts outlined in this document, XYZ Corporation will gain greater acceptance of its new XYZ Salt Substitute with its network of independent sales representatives. Our agency has researched the needs of these representatives and has found a common element among them that will allow us to create a powerful sales and informational tool. This innovative tool will permit the average sales rep to utilize a previously wasted time segment for learning about and gaining enthusiasm for XYZ's Salt Substitute.

Once the sales reps are informed and excited about XYZ Salt Substitute, this very same sales tool will maintain the excitement and provide specialized techniques and procedures for selling greater quantities of the product. This sales tool will evolve with the needs of the sales reps.

Since the sales rep will be saving time while learning about this product, he or she will be more receptive to continuing special offers and promotions that are communicated with this sales tool.

Implementation

We believe that an audio newsletter, produced biweekly, is the best way to inform and excite the network of independent sales representatives responsible for the successful store and shelf placement for XYZ Salt Substitute. This audio newsletter will be produced on cassette, allowing the reps to listen to it while they are driving between appointments. Since our research has shown that the average rep spends over half of his or her work time in the car, we feel this is the perfect medium to distribute educational and motivational information about XYZ Salt Substitute.

The newsletter will be 30 to 45 minutes long and will be produced like a radio show. A few lifestyle tidbits (excellent fodder for water cooler conversation) will be used in each newsletter to increase the entertainment and "listenability" value. Transitions between segments will be marked by brief musical interludes.

Two professional narrators will be used, one male and one female. The two will work in tandem (not unlike a morning radio team) to deliver the information about XYZ Salt Substitute.

For the first few weeks, the thrust of our audio newsletter will be very motivational, using the facts about the increasing popularity of low-salt or salt-free foods and diets. Within a few weeks, the newsletter will take on a more informational (but still extremely entertaining) form. Updates on pricing and special promotions will also be delivered through the newsletters.

A hotline will be set up using a simple phone machine to record questions or comments from the reps. When appropriate, we will edit these questions (with the actual voice of the rep) into the audio newsletter. This will serve to personalize the medium, much the same way call-in requests are used on commercial radio stations.

Given the audio production resources of our agency, we will be able to write, produce and distribute the newsletter within a two day period. That means the information will be right up-to-the-minute. Any sudden changes in pricing, strategy, etc., will be communicated in just a few days. Although a FAX or overnight letter could be used to send the information faster than this, the unique nature of the audio newsletter will virtually guarantee your message will be heard *and* understood.

Success stories of sales representatives who have excelled at the placement of XYZ Salt Substitute will be used in later editions of the audio newsletter. Like all aspects of this sales tool, these stories will be brief and uplifting.

This audio newsletter will increase sales for XYZ Salt Substitute by educating and motivating the independent sales representatives responsible for selling the product.

Cost

The cost for the increased market penetration and sales for XYZ Salt Substitute through the use of an audio newsletter is detailed below:

One year of writing, producing and distributing 300 audio newsletters every other week (26 weeks per year), a total of 7800 tapes will cost $19.50 per tape. This is less than the cost of sending two overnight letters to your sales representative each week. The total cost equals $8250 per week, based on a one year contract of $152,100. This amount may be paid in full within 30 days of the date this agreement is accepted and signed. It may also be paid quarterly, with installments of $38,025 due every three months for one year.

This total cost covers all aspects of research, writing (including a one day approval stage for XYZ Corporation), audio production, talent fees, tape duplication and distribution (by overnight delivery).

In addition to the 300 copies duplicated for the field every other week, XYZ Corporation will receive an additional 10 copies for intercompany use.

Delivery

Our agency will handle *all* aspects of delivery and distribution for this audio newsletter. All charges are based on a two day approval of written copy by XYZ Corporation. Should any approval cycle exceed two days, any necessary express delivery and rush production charges will be billed as they are incurred. Complete documentation of these additional charges will be provided before billing.

Summary

The biweekly audio newsletter proposed in this document will increase the sales of XYZ Salt Substitute by motivating and informing independent sales representatives about this new product. Since this information is presented in an easy-to-use format (audio cassette), XYZ's independent reps will listen to and comprehend the information while driving to their various appointments.

The product will be fresh in their minds as they meet with various food store managers and executives. This will help them to present it in an exciting and informed manner, helping them to make an effective case for preferential shelf space for the new product (the toughest hurdle for any new product).

The cost to receive the benefits of this biweekly newsletter for one year is less than sending each sales rep two express letters per week for the same period.

Acceptance

We, the undersigned, agree to the terms set forth in this proposal document. We also agree that we are empowered by XYZ Corporation to make the decision to use an audio newsletter to increase awareness and enthusiasm for XYZ Salt Substitute.

Name: Date Signed:

_____   _____

_____   _____

_____   _____

The final section, ACCEPTANCE, is vital to the success of any proposal document. I have seen many proposals that have no way for the customer to agree to the sale. Sure, he or she could make a phone call, but you're adding an extra step and giving them time for "buyer's remorse" to set in.

Additionally, the ACCEPTANCE section spells out, in a non-threatening, matter-of-fact way, that the people signing the agreement *have* the power to sign it. In those rare instances where there are any future hassles with the project, this section can save you a great deal of trouble.

The XYZ Salt Substitute Proposal worked. The customer agreed to the idea within 48 hours of receiving the document. The idea itself worked extremely well. Sales for the company's product increased enough that we were hired as their permanent ad agency, a deal that brought more than $500,000 per year.

Sample Sales Letter

Like proposals, sales letters come in all shapes and sizes. When you're trying to sell through a letter, your text, like a direct mail piece, must intrigue your customer with how the benefits of your product will specifically apply to them. Like direct mail copy, you only have a few seconds to do this. Remember, most people sort their mail standing (or sitting) over a wastebasket. You have to make every second count!

I received the following letter while working as a creative director for an advertising agency. True, it is a letter from someone seeking employment as a copywriter, but her grasp of using The Benefit of The Benefit really struck me — enough to save the letter for more than ten years!

Sara Smith
1302 Any Street
Cleveland, OH
216-555-5555

Steve Bryant
Creative Director
Corporate Creativity
1802 Sandalwood
Atlanta, GA
Dear Steve,

How would you like to have all your copywriting assignments finished ahead-of-schedule? I'll bet that would have helped you with the recent series of print ads you created for ABC Real Estate in Atlanta. It was a beautifully written campaign, I wish I would have had the chance to work on it with you. In the future, imagine increasing your profitability on similar projects by saving valuable writing time — time that could be spent on other profitable assignments.

That's just one of the benefits Corporate Creativity will receive by hiring me as your new head copywriter. In my five years with one of Cleveland's top agencies, I've never missed a deadline. Rather, my skill and efficiency as a writer have allowed me to finish my writing assignments well in advance of all deadlines. In fact, the head of my department, Sam Jones, will attest to this.

Speed is just one of my attributes. My projects always met or surpassed my client's needs and goals. My print campaign for some local hardware stores was so successful that it was adopted by their national chain. It's still used today. I have many specific client references that I will be glad to show you in a personal interview.

While I have been happy working with my company in Cleveland, they cannot provide the challenge or opportunities I require as my talent and expertise continue to grow. They are aware of my job search and my department head, Sam Jones, will be happy to answer any questions about my writing abilities and skill as a team player. Feel free to contact him or any other company principal. The telephone number is 216-555-5555.

Steve, no letter can properly convey the comprehensive nature of my abilities as well as my desire to work with you and your team at Corporate Creativity. I will call you in a few days to set up an appointment so we can discuss the possibilities in person.

Let's win together!

Sincerely,

Sara Smith

Whew! This one still boggles my imagination. She stressed how her talents would have applied to a recent ad campaign we had done (which emphasized the specific benefits of hiring her). This job had received a small amount of publicity in some trade journals, so she really had to dig to find out about it. She obviously had done her homework and her writing style hit a homerun.

Did I hire her? I tried, but she had sent out several such benefits-specific letters and another agency got to her first. But I still have her letter. If I ever need a job in the future, I full well intend to use this as a model for my own benefits-oriented "prospecting" letter.

Although I've urged you to use direct mail style as a guide to writing successful sales letters, there's one element that you should avoid, especially in a business-to-business letter. It's called The Johnson Box. Here's what it looks like:

Dear Customer,

****

You Can Have Greater Profits Tomorrow!

****

While segregating an opening benefit like this may work well for Ed McMahon and everyone else who's selling sweepstakes-based magazine subscriptions, I think you'll agree that it looks tacky in a professional business letter. But, if you're selling subscriptions to a publication like *The Journal of Professional Aardvark Lovers*...no, not even then.

Along with the Johnson Box, avoid cutesy graphics or phony URGENT pleas (extremely common in today's direct mail) on the envelope. You're not sending out millions of letters, hoping for a minimal return. You're sending out a personal letter that should look like just that. Many of the most successful direct mail campaigns had to go to great lengths to look like your simple, one page "personal" sales letter.

Written Comparisons

A written product comparison is another excellent way to show your customers The Benefits of The Benefits of owning your product. I'm not talking about something along the lines of those annoying commercials on radio and TV that claim one product is better than another. Do they insult your intelligence? Mine too.

The type of comparison I've found to be the most effective is what I call an "Apples-to-Apples" comparison. It works very well if you have several products that essentially do the same thing (camcorders, stereos, microwave ovens, cars, etc.). You create a Features/Benefits chart for all versions or models of the products you are selling. This chart makes it easy for your customer to see how the benefits of one product or model might better fit his or her individual needs.

For example, if you are selling camcorders, your customer has three basic formats from which to choose: Standard VHS, VHS-C and 8 Millimeter. Each one has its own advantages (and drawbacks). There is no *one* right choice for everyone. For example, 8MM camcorders have the best picture of all the formats. However, the 8MM units have some draw-backs (primarily non-compatibility with home VCRs). Do the benefits of this better picture quality outweigh the non-compatibility issue? It depends on the specific needs of your customer.

If you are dealing with customers who don't know a great deal about camcorders (and this is usually the case), you want to educate them first. Like the story of Sara (the electronics salesperson), related earlier in this book, you want to use your product knowledge to guide your customer to make the choice that's right for him or her.

As a salesperson, you have a lot riding on their decision. If a customer makes the wrong choice, you have made one sale but lost any word-of-mouth rec-ommendations that might have brought you addi-tional sales.

While you can make the "Apples-to-Apples" com-parison in a verbal presentation, the written word works better when you are selling a complex product with many benefits. It will take you a little time to create a convincing written document showing a pos-itive comparison between the benefits of different models, but this effort will pay off.

I created the following charts for a camcorder presentation on QVC. I had three camcorders to present, one in each format. In the course of an hour, I had to educate our customers so that they could make the right decision. I identified ten Features-to-Benefits aspects for owning a camcorder and wrote out the following charts. I still receive mail from viewers who are grateful I took the time to clarify the differences between the formats. Most of this mail

Sample Comparison Charts
Which Camcorder is Right For You?

Sharp Slimcam Full Size VHS

Features	Benefits
1. Smallest/lightest full size VHS	Comfort
2. Compatibility with home VCR	Convenience
3. State-of-the-art autofocus system	Better action and sports videos
4. Advanced auto exposure system	Superior color in sun and shadows
5. Easy to carry on shoulder	Stable videos (less shaking)
6. 1 lux rating	Excellent videos in all lighting conditions
7. Flying erase head	Perfect transitions
8. 12x1 zoom lens	Great close-up and candid videos
9. Advanced editing capabilities	Professional look-ing, more interest-ing videos
10. Automatic date	Accurate record keeping

JVC Compact VHS

Features	Benefits
1. Smallest/lightest VHS-C	Great for travel
2. Compatibility with home VCR	Convenience (playpack included)
3. Through The Lens autofocus	Clear videos
4. Auto exposure system	Good color indoors and out
5. Carry & shoot like a still camera	Quick response to all shooting opportunities
6. 1 lux rating	Excellent videos in all lighting conditions
7. Flying erase head	Perfect transitions
8. 6x1 zoom	Good close-up and candid videos
9. Basic editing capabilities	More interesting videos
10. Automatic birthday/date	Most accurate record keeping

Chinon Pocket 8 (8MM)

Features	Benefits
1. Smallest/lightest camcorder on QVC	Best for extensive travel
2. Best image quality	Superior video copies
3. Through The Lens autofocus	Clear videos
4. Auto exposure system	Good color indoors and out
5. Carry and shoot like a still camera	Quick response to all shooting opportunities
6. 3 lux rating	Good videos in all lighting conditions
7. Flying erase head	Perfect transitions
8. 6x1 zoom lens	Good close-up and candid videos
9. Basic editing capabilities	More interesting videos
10. Automatic date	Accurate record keeping

Notice that all the Features-to-Benefits correlations are made in an extremely positive manner. There's no "this is better than that" type of comparison. The Benefits are worded to show their specific application to the needs of various customers.

#1 shows the customer how the sizes of the three camcorders fit into his or her lifestyle.

#2 lets the customer know when the improved image quality of 8MM will be an important factor.

In #3, the primary benefit of the Sharp Slimcam's advanced autofocus system is shown, without degrading the less effective autofocus systems of the other two units.

Likewise in #4, although the Slimcam has a superior exposure system, this superiority is noted without debasing the less advanced systems of the other two units.

The methods of carrying the camcorder addressed in #5 targets the specific desires of the customer. The full-size Slimcam provides the most stable image, while the other two offer an enhanced readiness factor.

Although the 1 lux rating of the Slimcam and JVC units noted in #6 offers better quality low light videos, the 3 lux of the Chinon 8MM is shown to be nearly as effective. (Honestly, the difference between 1 and 3 lux is minimal, at best.)

In #7, the customer learns that all three camcorders offer the same smooth transitions between scenes.

The 12x1 zoom lens of the Slimcam highlighted in #8 offers the customer the ability to get twice as close to a subject as the 6x1 lenses of the other two units. Notice how this is defined as *great for the Slimcam, but still good for the other two.* If great close-ups and candids are the most important benefit of owning a camcorder to the customer, then the Slimcam is the right choice.

(Sears pioneered this technique with their *good, better, best,* breakdown for different models of the same product. *Good* isn't bad, but if you need it and can afford it, wouldn't you rather have the *best?* And buying *better* indicates that you are moving up in the world. It's a brilliant concept.)

Similarly, in #9 the customers can make a decision based on their editing needs. If they will be doing a great deal of editing, then the Slimcam is again the right choice. Still, the other two are shown to have the basic editing capabilities needed by the average consumer.

Finally, if the customer is interested in keeping accurate records of when a video is taken, then the JVC unit is the best choice.

Keep in mind that I'm not suggesting you hand your customers this kind of document and let them read it by themselves. They might decide to take it with them to the next store or salesperson. Even when I showed these charts on QVC, I took the time to explain the separate points. It worked very well. The show was one of the most successful camcorder hours we've ever had on QVC.

Selling With The Written Word — Summary

You've seen that proposals and sales letters are excellent tools in all sales situations. A simple proposal or letter can help to sell retail goods and/or services along with high ticket business-to-business products.

All sales proposals and letters should begin by detailing how the benefits of your product specifically apply to your customer (Benefits of The Benefits). An excellent way to see this in action is to study direct mail letters and ad campaigns.

A successful business proposal should be based around the following form:

1. *Specific Benefits* — targeted directly at your customer.

2. *Treatment (or) Implementation* — telling your customer what you are proposing to generate these benefits.

3. *Cost* — how much it will cost your customer to receive the benefits you've outlined. A favorable comparison with a known expense is a good way to buffer a seemingly high price.

4. *Delivery Options* — (if applicable) giving your customer a choice of normal or rush delivery, making sure the rush charges provide a sufficient profit for your company for the additional amount of work and expenses incurred.

5. *Summary* — a *brief* synopsis of the benefits of your product as well as a (soft) recapitulation of cost, again using a comparison to a known cost factor (if possible) to soften what might appear to be a greater-than-expected expense.

6. *Acceptance* — always give your customer an *easy* way to say yes. Also include some copy that identifies the people signing the document as the proper decision makers.

Sales letters, like proposals, should begin with the specific benefits of your product. A successful sales letter should be no more than one page and should flow in a conversational style similar to a personal letter.

Even though direct mail letters are excellent guidelines for sales letters and proposals, you shouldn't duplicate their hard-edged graphic style. Doing this can destroy the personal touch you are trying to establish, especially in a letter.

Written comparisons can help your customers take an active role in identifying how the benefits of different models of the same product specifically apply to them. This type of chart should show all the differences between models in a positive light. A comparison chart will have the greatest impact if you take the time to explain it.

Don't underestimate the power of selling with the written word in all sales situations. A powerful benefits-packed letter, proposal or chart might be all it takes to set you and your product apart from the crowd. And, as you've seen from this section, the only magic involved in successful sales writing is the magic of innovation, determination and hard work.

Communica-tions

O kay, maybe the title of this section is a little all-encompassing, but realize that bad internal or external communications can destroy the best sales efforts. The old adage *"never let your left hand know what your right hand is doing"* was not written by a salesperson...at least not a very good one.

Internal communications — the sharing of information between people playing on the same team — is crucial to the development of the basic concepts and ideas that are the building blocks of an effective sales presentation. Whether you are selling one-on-one at the retail level or making multi-million dollar corporate sales pitches, the internal communications within your organization can make or break you.

Training, or the lack thereof, is probably the chief offender in the world of bad internal communications. In this first section, I'll address how to *get* the training you need. Knowing how to *get* the right training is more important than understanding the proper techniques needed to *give* a training session. Most trainees don't think they can control the information they are receiving from an "experienced" trainer. They're wrong!

Getting the Training You Need

While there are some great trainers in the world, they seem to be the exception. Bad trainers abound. I'm sure you've yawned your way through as many dull ersatz training meetings as I have. I call these ineffective educational enclaves ersatz because they really are false, bearing no resemblance to true training. Good training gives you the information you need to focus in on specific benefits of the product you are selling.

I can't believe how many times I've been in bad training meetings where the majority of the salespeople (myself included) were content to simply endure the tedium. We left the meeting no smarter than we were when it started. In fact, there were times when I felt like I had lost valuable brain cells during one of these interminable training snafus. (After 40, you don't have that many to spare.)

So what can you do to insure you aren't bored out of your socks by a trainer who's about as interesting as spackle? Like Peter Finch in the movie *Network,* get "mad as hell and don't take it anymore!"

One day, while attending a well-rehearsed, canned training session, I realized I had had enough. The trainer was giving information on some shoes we would be selling on QVC. She was nervous and called everyone in the meeting "Sugarbumps." Her patter was absolutely stock! Even though the information we required was far different than what the average retail salesperson needed, she was giving us the same retail pitch she had been using for years.

I hadn't seen that many flip charts since John Kennedy explained the Cuban Missile Crisis on TV back in 1962. When I raised my hand to ask a question that might help us to determine the specific benefits of her product as they applied to *our* customers, she paused for several moments and asked me to hold my question for the end of the session. She then backtracked to a point in her presentation she had made a few minutes before and started churning out the same drivel. I was so bored I began to see if I could remember all the cast names in *Car 54, Where Are You?* It helped — I didn't fall asleep and did list everyone's name except the guy who played the Captain.

Once she had finished, I repeated my question ("What's the profile of your average customer — age, career, interests?") She told me she didn't know and that I shouldn't concentrate on such specifics, these were comfortable, good looking shoes that *everyone* would love (a classic case of believing your own Public Relations). When I pressed her for an answer, my superior stepped in and reminded me that we had a lot of other trainers scheduled that day and if I had any specific questions, I should ask the lady in private. Okay, so trying to change training philosophy (or the lack thereof) *during* a meeting is probably bad form (and certainly bad timing).

Am I being too hard on this poor lady? I don't think so. Her shoes didn't sell very well, mostly because none of us had the information we needed to make an effective, Benefits of The Benefits type presentation.

There is a solution to bad training. It takes some guts and initiative, but when you think of the valuable time it will save, time that you can use for planning and delivering effective sales presentations, it's worth the hassle. Here's how it should work:

Take the time and the enterprise to establish written guidelines for your training requirements. Include all the information you need to create a convincing sales presentation to your customers. Make the document as formal and polished as possible and then present it to the people responsible for setting up training sessions in your company.

I've found it's best to structure this document like a sales proposal. And why not? You're literally selling a new idea to management. Like me, you may experience some initial resistance to this tactic. Still, if you show your management team the Benefits of The Benefits of adopting your ideas, they'll usually come around to your way of thinking.

Once adopted by management, make sure these guidelines are sent to all trainers well in advance of any future sessions. Include a letter asking the trainers to respond to your suggestions. If you get a negative response, saying something like "Our training has always proven itself to be effective in the past," or some similar retort, contact this company immediately.

Whoever does this will have to put on his or her best sales persona to try to get the "inflexible" company to yield. If they continue to refuse to tailor their training to your needs, maybe you'd do better to cancel the session, or even rethink selling the product in question.

Establishing these training guidelines will benefit you in several ways. First of all, by identifying the information you and your sales peers need to sell a product, you've already established a formula for finding The Benefits of The Benefits for the product. Even if your guidelines are ignored by management, they will help you in your future sales efforts.

Secondly, this effort will show your management team that *you* are several cuts above average. Not too many people would take the time to create this training guideline. Extra efforts like this play very well when annual reviews come around. This is especially true since the results of more effective training will be evident in the increased sales that are generated.

(Author's note: If extra efforts like this are repeatedly ignored by your company, GET OUT! Start sending resumes, making calls, pulling in favors, etc. Do whatever it takes to get with a company that has a more creative environment. This advice comes from personal experience. I have worked for two companies that actually discouraged this type of thing. Their "that's the way we've always done it" philosophy was the kiss of death. Both of these firms no longer exist, but I got out before their corporate ships went down.)

Many of you might be asking, "Why should I help to establish guidelines that will aid other salespeople?" I've heard that sentiment expressed by many salespeople. Although they were highly motivated individuals, their "separatist" attitudes prevented them from becoming truly successful. They were afraid that by helping their peers to succeed, their own goals were threatened.

Whether you're creating training guidelines for your company, or simply helping a peer develop a more focused sales approach for a specific customer, *never* hesitate to help a fellow salesperson. Your thoughtfulness will be repaid many times over, even if it's only in the way people perceive you. I'm not saying to neglect your own efforts, but it's been my experience that the help you give another salesperson on your team will eventually benefit you in ways you might never have expected.

Get the training you need. Demand it! Take control of the situation and create your own curriculum. You'll save time and have the information you need to be a more effective salesperson.

A Magical Interlude

Harry Houdini (a/k/a Eric Weiss) perfected an older illusion called Metamorphosis where the magician changed places with someone who was bound and locked in a trunk. Harry had to interview several magicians around the world to find out enough about the effect to perfect it, so the change would be instantaneous. After he discovered a way to do this, he performed this mind boggling deception with such skill that it consistently astounded audiences around the globe.

Sir Arthur Conan Doyle, the creator of Sherlock Holmes and one of the leading analytical minds of the day, reviewed the performance for the London Times. He wrote that Houdini must have discovered a way to dissolve the molecules of his body as well as that of his assistant in order to make such an immediate transposition. Doyle firmly held this belief until the day he died.

Training Penetration (Assume Nothing)

While there are some great books on setting up an effective training program, most lack one vital element. This is a factor I refer to as *Training Penetration*. The best training program in the world will flop if the information doesn't *penetrate* to the people who need it the most. If you are setting up any type of training to help people sell a product you are selling them, *Training Penetration* is essential.

Most training seminars given to management personnel usually contain a great deal of useful information for non-management employees as well. Too many times, managers absorb and utilize the information they are given with no thought of disseminating it to the "troops in the field." They *assume* that since they were trained, the information they now possess will filter down through through their actions (osmosis?).

One of my favorite Red Skelton characters (on both radio and TV) was "The Mean Wittle Kid." This nasty child was supposedly given too many vitamins in the hospital, causing him to be the size of an adult. It made for a very funny bit to hear all the doctors and nurses prattling, "I gave him his vitamins." "No, *I* gave him his vitamins!" "You're all wrong, *I* gave him his vitamins!!!"

Finally, in unison, they all chanted "Oh no, we *all* gave him his vitamins!" At this point, an adult-sized child appeared. Despite the medical implausibility of the entire idea, the scenario was hysterically funny. However, this example of bad communications is all too often replayed, with disastrous results, in the world of sales.

Never assume! The old adage, *When you assume, you make an ass out of u and me* is especially true in sales. Let me give you an example:

One of the country's leading designers and manufacturers of costume jewelry recently created a line of "fakes" based on jewelry owned by a rather fashionable member of Britain's Royal Family. The designer is world renowned for creating some of the world's finest costume jewelry. His creations are regarded as the Rolls Royce of fashion jewelry. They are worn by the "Who's Who" in the worlds of show business and high fashion.

This new line was highly publicized in fashion magazines and trade publications. It was touted as one of the most important lines of fake jewels ever created.

A major department store was given the exclusive rights to debut the jewelry in this country. Breathtaking jewelry at an affordable price — the line had all the earmarks of a sales monster. However, even with all the hoopla, the line got off to a less than auspicious start.

When sales for the jewelry were far less than expected, the designer decided to do a little snooping. He had one of his people go to a main branch of the chain and inquire about an attractive window display for the jewelry. The store employee replied "I don't know, let me find out."

After making several phone calls, the store employee was told (by someone in *authority*) that the gorgeous pieces of jewelry in the window were just for display...**Not for sale!???**

I must commend the person for remaining so calm at this response. Maybe he realized that this bad information, caused by a lack of *Training Penetration*, could really be traced back to his company. Needless to say, the feces really hit the fan. It seems that the designer's company had *assumed* that giving the necessary information to the store's management team was sufficient. Although the information was complete, most of it never filtered down to the retail salespeople...the obvious front line in any retail sales effort.

After the initial brouhaha died down, the company that designed and manufactured the jewelry made it their business to get the information on this new line to *everybody* responsible for selling it. They even conducted thorough training seminars specifically for the retail clerks.

Although these improved communications did increase sales for the jewelry, the initial impact for the line was lost. It did well (and continues to do so), but who knows what kind of results would have been achieved if the proper communications channels were in place from the beginning?

A Magical Interlude

Harry Blackstone Sr. would be very proud to see how his son, Harry Jr., has elevated the art of magic. Harry Jr.'s stage show is one of the most popular magic acts in the world today. One of his signature pieces, The Floating Light Bulb, has been mystifying audiences for decades.

As the name implies, a "regular" lit bulb floats from Harry's hands and travels through the theater. The bulb has no means of support and Harry can direct it to float to anyone in the audience. However, before Harry allows it to "visit" someone, he always tells the person not to touch the bulb or they'll break the spell. He doesn't make one "blanket" announcement to the crowd. Rather, he gently reminds every person about the no touching proviso, making sure that every person who needs the information gets it. In all the times I've seen this beautiful illusion, no one has ever reached for the bulb.

Bad Training Penetration can show up in all aspects of the sales process, in any business. Sometimes, your efforts can be torpedoed by someone you never even thought was a part of the sales team. Check out the following example:

I recently went to a new local restaurant. It was part of an upscale national chain known for its great Italian food and fast service. I walked in and the hostess was not at the welcoming desk. However, the cashier was behind the register. She was writing out the evening's specials on a blackboard. Although she saw my party as we walked in, she continued to write out the specials and said nothing to us.

It took the hostess almost five minutes to return to the front of the restaurant and notice that we were waiting. We would have left if it hadn't been brutally cold outside, making any thoughts of returning to the car most unpleasant.

The hostess apologized, explaining that she was dealing with a minor crisis in the kitchen (not an explanation that inspired a great deal of confidence in the quality of the food to come, but that's a whole different marketing mistake). As she was seating us, I inquired about why the cashier hadn't at least told us that she would be a few minutes. "That's not her job," the hostess politely announced.

"But she could have at least acknowledged our presence," I replied.

"I guess," the hostess said, "but it's really not her job."

It's not her job...it's not my department...How many times have we all had to put up with that nonsense? Anyway, after the initial debacle service was fine and dinner was most enjoyable.

Still, the words "it's not her job" were echoing through my mind. I decided to speak to the manager of the restaurant, to confirm what I already suspected. I asked the manager if it was policy to train the service staff. He assured me that since the chain prided itself on great customer service, all hostesses, waiters and waitresses received a three day on-site seminar on effective customer service techniques.

"What about the cashiers?" I asked.

"We train them in the proper use of the register," he noted. "They have to pass a math test before they're allowed to handle money."

"No service training?" I asked.

(Although you probably know what's coming, rest assured that it's just about an exact quote from the manager.) "It's really not their job," he replied.

I realized what a good example this would be to show the effect of bad Training Penetration. A little customer service training and this cashier, *the first person you usually see in this restaurant,* would have been a valuable asset to the establishment's marketing efforts. How well is your FPOC (First Point Of Contact) trained in the proper techniques of customer service? A bad first impression can destroy even the finest sales efforts.

As proof of this, realize that when someone asks for a restaurant recommendation in the future, all I'll remember is the bad service I experienced at this place. I've already forgotten what I had for dinner.

The bad initial service has killed any hope of word-of-mouth advertising they might have received from me.

There are some simple ways to make sure your training penetrates to all levels of an organization, regardless of who personally attends your training sessions. The enormously successful Mary Kay organization has developed one of the most effective methods for doing this.

Mary Kay has approximately 250,000 consultants worldwide. Clearly, this makes one humongous training session out of the question. Mary Kay does provide solid, on-going training for its over 5,000 sales directors, but the company doesn't stop there. They produce a slick, full color monthly magazine, titled *Applause,* for their quarter-million worldwide troops. This publication recaps *all t*he information given to the directors in their personal training sessions.

Mary Kay's Directors do more than most corporate executives to provide their minions with the information they need to make focused, benefits-oriented sales presentations. However, *Applause* makes sure that Mary Kay's front line salespeople have all the information they need right at their fingertips. It's an excellent form of printed reinforcement. *Applause* also features motivational stories on different consultants each month, helping to ensure that the publication gets a thorough reading.

If you are setting up a training program, try this type of reinforcement for the lower level employees who won't have the opportunity to attend your sessions personally. If a full color magazine is a little out of your reach, a simple typed newsletter will do the trick. An audio newsletter, like the one detailed in the section on written sales presentations, is also an excellent medium for reaching those who are unable to attend your training sessions.

Make the people who cannot attend your training sessions feel special while getting them the information they need. Once they know you consider them to be important, they'll do more to help sell your product.

If you are selling a product that will be resold by a salesforce, then you should get that product into the hands of the people who are selling it. Payola? Not at all. For decades, car dealerships have allowed their salespeople to use the cars they are selling as their own. Once they have lived with the vehicle for a while, they are better able to identify its specific benefits to different types of customers.

One of my favorite examples of this technique involves an unassuming little product offered on QVC. It's a man's necktie called Tie Button Tie. The tie buttons to your shirt with a patented slider mechanism that keeps it in place at all times. A great idea, but even I wondered how any of us were going to be able to create eight minutes of exciting TV simply talking about a necktie.

The creator of the ties, a very sharp entrepreneur named Vincent Pileggi, gave one of the most powerful training sessions I've ever attended. Instead of giving us "The History of Men's Neckwear," he briefly showed us how the ties worked and promptly gave each of us several of them to wear.

It worked! Our personal experiences with the ties enabled each of us to create convincing sales presentations based on The Benefits of The Benefits of owning the ties. Instead of having to recall the copious notes we took during an interminable training session, we all had personal experiences with the product. Tens of thousands of Tie Button Ties have been sold and they continue to do very well.

Giving (or sometimes even lending) your product to salespeople can be tricky. Many companies have strict guidelines about their employees accepting gifts from vendors. But, if getting your product into the hands of the people selling it is okay with the powers that be, go for it! The individual experiences the salespeople have with your product will translate into some very impressive sales.

Meeting Head On

Another important aspect of communications is the sales meeting. Whether it's the big annual sales conference or a local get-together, a meeting with your peers can be one of the most valuable sales aids for everyone concerned. Unfortunately, many sales meetings that I've attended have been boring and virtually pointless.

The most common mistakes people make when setting up a meeting are the reasons for having the meeting in the first place. Regular weekly meetings can be a real waste of time. Meeting because "we always meet on Thursdays" is stupid. If you have no information to share, then scheduling a meeting out of habit is completely counterproductive.

Breaking out of the "we have to meet on this day every week" mold is difficult. If company management is convinced that they would lose control over the sales staff if they don't meet with them on a frequent, regular basis, you'll have to tread very lightly.

The first thing to do is to take notes on all the important information that is discussed at the meeting. If there are several truly important points discussed, then there are obviously good reasons for having the meeting. If, on the other hand, you find that you've listed very few important points, you have your work cut out for you.

If you log several meetings in a row that prove to be unproductive, take the time to write up a proposal or letter for management. Detail the time required to cover the important information in the meetings. If you show that the information covered in three to four meetings would have been just as (if not more) effectively covered in one meeting, your management team should listen.

Your proposal or letter should be worded in the same type of benefits-oriented style featured in the sample proposal shown earlier in this book. Be careful! Don't come off sounding like a disgruntled salesperson or a know-it-all. Whoever reads your document will probably be the person responsible for setting up these meetings. In fact, depending upon the size of your company, scheduling and running these meetings may be his or her most important job. You have a good chance to make a powerful enemy.

You also have an excellent opportunity to make a very influential ally. If your proposal addresses things like "more efficient methods for establishing The Benefits of The Benefits for your company's products," your words are likely to fall on more receptive ears. Show, through example if possible, how condensing or eliminating some meetings will give the sales force more time to sell without any loss of information or control.

As an alternative to face-to-face meetings, propose a sales-specific newsletter. (If I seem hell-bent on this type of thing, it's because I've never seen a well written and produced newsletter that didn't have a measurable, positive impact.) This newsletter would include new product information, customer updates and all the other facts that are usually covered in a regular meeting.

Offer your assistance with the newsletter project, but don't make it sound like you will do most of the work. If that happens, you'll wish you were back in the non-productive meetings which took a lot less time than producing the entire document you're proposing.

Suggest that the person currently responsible for the meetings serve as an editor for the newsletter. Also note that the bulk of the writing should be done by a combination of salespeople and company communications people.

Make sure that you indicate this newsletter is not intended to replace *all* meetings. You should propose that the newsletter be used as a supplement to the meeting process, eliminating perhaps half the regularly scheduled encounters.

If you meet with resistance, push only as hard as you would with an indecisive customer. Any more pressure on your part could brand you as a rebel.

Whether your sales meetings are productive or not, one way to increase (or establish) their productivity is to have a portion of the meeting time devoted to identifying new benefits and Benefits of Benefits for your company's products. These brain-storming sessions can make active participants out of the quietest people.

Imagine; a serious, productive exchange of ideas, where everyone will undoubtedly learn something new. Your peers may have identified benefits of the products your company sells that might never have occurred to you and vise versa. This ongoing give-and-take is exactly the kind of thing that makes you anxious to go to a meeting.

Capitalize on the individual strengths of your peers. Every member of your sales team has a different expertise. One person may know more about the technical aspect of your products than anyone else. Another may have great customer insights. Still another might have identified a unique product application. Use these differences to unite your sales effort.

At every meeting, have a different member give a *brief* presentation about his or her area(s) of product or customer expertise. Sure, it's extra work, but I'll bet very few will complain. I've worked for a few companies who have done this type of information exchange on a regular basis. You should see the person who is going to give a presentation on the day of the meeting. They're a lot like a kid giving a first book report. They're usually really frightened about talking in front of their peers...frightened but exhilarated at the opportunity to "show their stuff."

Once everyone has had a turn at giving a presentation, then it should be voluntary...for a while. If no one volunteers for the next couple of meetings, then your meeting leader should listen very carefully during your brainstorming sessions for any new ideas. When an innovative idea is unearthed in one of the sessions dedicated to finding new Benefits of The Benefits, the person responsible for the idea should be asked to dig deeper into the subject for the next get-together.

In addition to these brainstorming sessions, sales meetings should be open to *any* discussions related to selling product. Agendas are fine, but closing out any new idea simply because it wasn't on the schedule will kill creativity and, eventually, sales. An open meeting atmosphere is crucial to having effective and enjoyable meetings.

I'm sure many of you are wondering what this "open meeting" concept does to the length of most meetings. Sure, it makes them longer, but the added length is *productive* length. So how long does a meeting have to be before it gets counterproductive? It varies, but this is a rather complex issue.

Sometimes the person putting the meeting together believes that you *must* meet every week and each meeting *must* run for a minimum length (that's a lethal combination of *musts*). We've all seen these meetings scheduled between the hours of 1:00 and 3:00 PM. Does that make your skin crawl like mine? Heaven help you if the meeting is over early or runs late. I've even been in sessions where the meeting leader said, "Well, we're done, but it's too early to let you go. Why don't you take the next few minutes to read over your notes and we'll break this up in about 20 minutes." (The guy got out alive — go figure.)

Conversely, we've also attended meetings where the person in charge said something like, "It's too nice a day to stay cooped up inside. Let's just cover the basics and hit the golf course."

While most of us would rather be at the latter gathering, neither approach is correct. You are meeting for a purpose. When that purpose is fulfilled, then the meeting is over (unless it's a really nice day and the golf course is across the street and you just happen to have your clubs in the trunk...).

If your meetings are suffering from too rigid or too loose a schedule, speak to the person in charge or, better yet, write out a benefits-oriented proposal or letter addressing the needs of you and your peers. And, if you run into serious opposition, again push only as hard as you would with an indecisive customer. Keep your good standing with the company while you do what it takes to "get out and get out fast." A company who won't listen to ways to improve its own performance is doomed. I've been there.

Communicate, share information, make sure everyone (including you) has the knowledge he or she needs to *sell*.

A Final Magical Interlude

Magicians sharpen their skills with magic books, instructional video tapes, one-on-one lessons and by attending magic conventions. In fact, hundreds of conventions are held throughout the country each year. Most of these gatherings boast an impressive roster of experts who teach different types of magic in intimate seminar settings. It's interesting to note that while these teaching sessions are important, they aren't always the primary medium for the exchange of information.

At any magic convention, you will see attendees sharing their own individual expertise with one another during impromptu get-togethers throughout the convention. Many times, these unscheduled sessions prove to be better environments for the exchange of information than the formally scheduled classes.

Communications Summary

Getting the training you need is equally as important as giving an effective training seminar. To get the training required to create a more focused sales presentation, you should provide the trainer with guidelines detailing the information you need. This can be done through a benefits-oriented proposal submitted to the person in your company responsible for setting up these training sessions.

When you are training salespeople who will be reselling the product you are selling them, *Training Penetration* is vital. If your training doesn't penetrate to *all* levels of an organization, the sales of your product will suffer. This is especially true if you're dealing with retail sales, where the actual salespeople are usually at the bottom of the corporate ladder.

To ensure that your training information gets to everyone who needs it, consider producing a magazine or a written or audio newsletter for those who cannot attend your training in person.

Another extremely powerful way to communicate the specific benefits of your product to the people who are reselling it is to give them the product. Not only will they be grateful for the freebie, but they'll have a much better understanding of the product's benefits from personal experience.

Sales meetings are most effective if you meet *only when there's a reason to exchange information.* If your company has regularly scheduled meetings that seem unproductive, suggest (in a proposal or letter) that they consider scheduling meetings less frequently. Propose a newsletter written especially for the salesforce as an alternative to regular meetings.

Open brainstorming sessions, especially those involving the identification of new Benefits of The Benefits for your products, are a fine way to maximize meeting results. Encourage members of your sales team to make presentations on their individual areas of product and customer expertise.

Having a set length for a meeting is as ineffective as having regularly scheduled meetings when there is no sales-related reason to meet. Meetings should be as long (or short) as necessary to be effective.

Poor communications and ineffective meetings are like bad magicians. You'll never forget them...but you'll want to.

Conclusion

Showing your customer how the benefits of your product specifically apply to him or her will help you to boost sales. It's as simple as that. The Benefits of The Benefits of any product or service will be different to every customer. Defining them will let your customers know that you have put in the extra effort necessary to understand exactly what they need. Their respect for you and your product will show up in increased sales now as well as in the future.

While this book has detailed many ways to identify and communicate specific benefits to your customer, it is really a work in progress. Like you, I'm forever refining my selling techniques, trying new things and "pushing the envelope." It may be trite, but I do keep a journal of ideas (where this book was "born") to have immediate access of which new ideas work and which ones were theoretical Edsels.

Explore all the techniques in this book and then dwarf them by defining how the benefits of these ideas specifically apply to you. Like a fine chef, use the "recipes" in the book as a guideline for your own imagination. You'll cook up some incredible results.

Selling is hard work, but *salespeople are the highest compensated professionals in the workforce today.* If you're willing to do the work, start planning how you're going to deal with the success, because it *will* come. I've never known a hardworking salesperson who wasn't worthy of the all envy he or she received.

I hope you get to know how damn good some **real magic** feels!

Index

Sales Magic Seminars

Create *Sales Magic* for your company! Reserve a Steve Bryant training seminar now!

In a training session tailored to your company's individual needs, Steve will:

- Show your salespeople how to easily identify The Benefits of The Benefits for your products or services.
- Teach your staff how to combine powerful marketing techniques into their everyday sales activities.
- Motivate your sales team to win and give them the tools to do it.
- Create new excitement for all your products!
- Establish new standards of excellence for everyone involved in the sales process.

Stop losing sales now! Give your company the advantage of The Benefit of The Benefit along with all the other proven strategies, concepts and techniques of *Sales Magic* before your competition beats you to it!

For a free seminar information packet, write to:

Amherst Media
PO Box 586
Amherst, NY 14226
Attn: Sales Magic Seminars